BIG FEELINGS

DEVOTIONS

FOR BOYS

BIG
FEELINGS
DEVOTIONS
FOR BOYS
WHAT GOD'S WORD
SAYS ABOUT EMOTIONS
BARBOUR kidz
A Division of Barbour Publishing

YOU are the reason we do what we do here at Barbour Publishing. We promise that we will always use our God-given talents to produce content with you in mind—and that we will remain biblically faithful, no matter what.

Thank you for being the heart of our business.

Print ISBN 979-8-89151-255-9

Published by Barbour Publishing, Inc., 1810 Barbour Drive, Uhrichsville, Ohio 44683, www.barbourbooks.com

Our mission is to inspire the world with the life-changing message of the Bible.

Printed in China.

002757 1225 HA

INTRODUCTION

Everyone has feelings. Some are linked to happiness and some to sadness. There are feelings that you enjoy, and then there are others you don't want to experience—not ever. Feelings can be confusing. And sometimes you might even need help managing them.

Boys like you make choices when they feel a certain way. But it's important to know that sometimes your feelings don't help you make great choices. For instance, if you're angry, you might make a choice that causes someone else to feel anger or hate too. That doesn't help anyone. Or you may feel love toward certain people in your life, and that can influence the way they feel about you.

Feelings aren't bad, but your feelings don't always tell the truth. For example, maybe you feel frustrated with someone, but you might not feel the same way if you knew the reason they do the things they do. Or sometimes you might feel scared, but really there's no reason to be afraid. Keep reading and explore the variety of emotions and what God has to say about each one.

YOUR HEART AND FEELINGS

"The heart is fooled more than anything else, and is very sinful. Who can know how bad it is?"
JEREMIAH 17:9 NLV

When the Bible talks about your heart, it's not talking about your physical heart. It refers to the place where all your feelings are stored—so you can get to them quickly. God lives there. Your heart is where important decisions are made. These decisions include both feelings and choices.

If someone does something mean to you, you might react with feelings of anger, frustration, or sadness. Dwelling on these feelings makes a person's meanness even meaner somehow. Your feelings tell you that what happened was unfair, so you think you should do something unfair in return. But God says these feelings can fool you. They'll make you believe you'll feel better by acting mean in return, but you won't. You might think a nasty comeback will make things better, but more likely it will make a bad situation even worse. God says to love others, but your emotions might tell you it would be better to hate instead. God says you should forgive, but feelings want you to make the choice to hold a grudge. When you make choices because of bad feelings, you'll often break God's rules.

THANKS FOR MY FEELINGS, LORD. HELP ME REMEMBER THEY'RE WORTH NOTICING BUT SOMETIMES GIVE VERY BAD ADVICE.

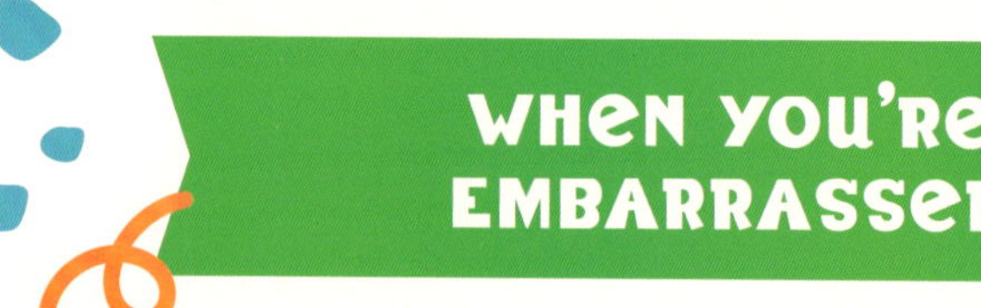

When You're Embarrassed

Work hard so you can present yourself to God and receive his approval. Be a good worker, one who does not need to be ashamed.
2 TIMOTHY 2:15 NLT

No one likes it when someone says, "You're wrong." You want to be right. That's when the feeling of embarrassment bubbles up in your heart.

God pays attention to you. When you do the right thing, He notices. When you make a wrong choice, He notices. Arguing with God doesn't work—because He's always right. When you do what He asks, you never need to be embarrassed or ashamed. When you break His rules, you should never tell God, "You're wrong." Admit He was right and take new steps with Him—He'll take away your embarrassment.

Embarrassment allows so many different feelings to have power over your choices. You might experience fear, jealousy, or even hate. None of these feelings tell others that you care about them.

I DON'T LIKE TO BE EMBARRASSED, FATHER. WHEN I SAY SOMETHING, IT'S BECAUSE I THINK I'M RIGHT. HELP ME BE WISE ENOUGH TO LEARN FROM YOU AND REFUSE TO LET EMBARRASSMENT LEAD ME TO MAKE BAD CHOICES.

GOD IS THE BEST CHOICE

I am not ashamed of the gospel, because it is the power of God that brings salvation to everyone who believes.

ROMANS 1:16 NIV

Do you remember reading that feelings don't always tell you the truth? Do you remember reading that being embarrassed might influence you to make bad choices?

You can listen to others who say that what God says isn't very important, and you can feel embarrassed because people notice that you follow Him. The feeling of embarrassment might influence you to make the choice to say that you don't love God or that you think He's not very important.

Embarrassment happens when someone catches you in a lie or when they question whether something you said was true. Both can feel like the end of the world. But you don't have to spend much time with embarrassment. Admit when you're wrong. Stand up for the truth. Never feel embarrassed for making God your best choice.

HELP ME NEVER FEEL EMBARRASSED BECAUSE I FOLLOW YOU, LORD. WHEN I KNOW YOU'RE RIGHT, HELP ME NEVER AGREE WITH OTHERS WHO SAY YOU'RE WRONG.

I can do all things

because Christ gives me

the strength.

BEWARE OF THE "WHAT IFS"

I can do all things because Christ gives me the strength.
PHILIPPIANS 4:13 NLV

Trying new things can be embarrassing. What if you're not very good at them? What if someone makes fun of you? What if other people do it better? That's a lot of what-ifs.

Most people won't try new things because they worry they might be embarrassed. But God can help you do hard things. The fact is, when you trust God enough to try new things, you might help other people trust Him too. Some of the things you may be challenged to do are really good ideas that make you feel nervous. But when you know that God wants you to do something, you don't need to be embarrassed to try. You'll always learn something in the process. You can be a good example too. Your feelings can be challenged to obey the God who asks you to do good things even when they're hard things.

YOU'RE A GOOD FATHER. HELP ME BE PATIENT AS I FOLLOW YOU, NOT LETTING MY FEELINGS GET IN THE WAY OF THE GOOD PLANS YOU HAVE FOR ME.

He Can Do It

We can say with confidence, "The LORD is my helper, so I will have no fear. What can mere people do to me?"
HEBREWS 13:6 NLT

When do you feel confident? Sometimes? Never? You might feel shy and would rather not be noticed. Or maybe you like people to notice you, and that means you try to make people think you're braver than you really are.

You might think that being brave and confident means you need big muscles and a loud voice. Some people think being confident means you make others feel embarrassed so you can look more important.

God says you should be confident, but that feeling should come from remembering that God is with you. He'll help you. No one is bigger than God. *No one.* Not you. Not the school bully. Not the strongest person you know. Feel confident because God can do what you can't, and He'll help when you struggle.

IT'S HARD TO FEEL CONFIDENT WHEN I'M EMBARRASSED, LORD. LET ME FEEL CONFIDENT BECAUSE YOU ARE WITH ME AND FOR ME.

GOOD THiNGS ARe COMiNG

Do not throw away your confidence; it will be richly rewarded. You need to persevere.
HEBREWS 10:35–36 NIV

You experience some feelings because of the choices you make. You might decide to show off, and that could lead to a feeling of embarrassment. Or you might decide to follow God, and that could lead to feelings of faith and assurance. Other feelings will try to get your attention, so you might be tempted to let go of your confidence while you spend time with unhelpful feelings like hurt, frustration, and anger. These are just a few of the feelings that can rob your confidence.

When you're confident in all the wonderful things God can do, you'll have a reward from Him. You might discover that you can talk about God more easily, and as you do, you'll grow in your ability to get rid of feelings that aren't helpful. God says the best thing you can do is persevere. That's a pretty big word, but it basically means to be patient while continuing to do the right things. Trust God that good things are coming!

WHY IS IT SO EASY TO GIVE UP, GOD? HELP ME BE CONFIDENT LONG ENOUGH TO SEE THE SURPRISING, WONDERFUL THINGS YOU WILL DO.

THiNGS AND STUFF

See those people polishing their chariots,
and those others grooming their horses?
But we're making garlands for GOD our God.
The chariots will rust, those horses pull up
lame—and we'll be on our feet, standing tall.
PSALM 20:7–8 MSG

You probably know people who own a lot of stuff that makes them feel important. Those things can make them feel confident, but owning things isn't where confidence comes from. Why? Well, things are just. . .*things*. If they break or if they are stolen, they might take your confidence and leave you with other feelings you wish you didn't have. Things you can own are never as important as God. When He gives you a feeling of confidence, it means that you know He can't be broken or taken away. Things will leave you feeling alone and lonely—God never does that!

God isn't just a good idea. He's the only place where real confidence can be found, and He's also the only one who never leaves you alone—not ever.

IT'S NICE TO HAVE THINGS THAT ARE MINE, FATHER.
BUT THINGS CAN NEVER BE MORE IMPORTANT
THAN MY FAMILY, FRIENDS, OR YOU.

GOD HELPS

We thought we would die. This happened so we would not put our trust in ourselves, but in God.
2 CORINTHIANS 1:9 NLV

When bad things happen, you probably don't think of yourself as confident. You certainly don't feel that way. You may not know why bad things are happening, and that can cause you to feel like making a bad choice will only make things worse. Then the feeling of fear comes along and invites worry as well. There's only one God you can trust. There's no need to trust yourself when you're paying attention to Him. Follow Him—it's always the right choice.

If you don't feel brave today, that's okay, because God is brave enough for every person who has ever lived. He will help you.

No trouble is so big that God can't take care of it. You'll always feel more confident when you remember that God helps those who ask Him for help.

WHEN I THINK THINGS ARE JUST TOO HARD, LORD, HELP ME REMEMBER YOU. BRING THE HELP I NEED SO I CAN FEEL CONFIDENT KNOWING I'M FOLLOWING THE BEST LEADER.

JUST WAIT

Wait patiently for the LORD. Be brave and courageous. Yes, wait patiently for the LORD.
PSALM 27:14 NLT

When you feel impatient, you often only think of things you *should* be doing—or things you *should* be trying. Waiting feels like you're wasting time—and it's hard to wait! When you're impatient, you think things aren't going the way they should.

Being impatient means you don't trust God to take care of things. But Psalm 27 says the best thing you can do is resist feeling impatient. Reach into your heart for the feeling of courage. Believe that God has a plan and that His plan is good. After all, He knows more about everything than you do.

You don't need to give in to the feeling of impatience. If God is willing to take care of things, then sit back and let Him do His thing. You can help by just watching Him do what only He can do.

IMPATIENCE ISN'T A GOOD FEELING, GOD. YOU KNOW HOW TO TAKE CARE OF ME BETTER THAN ANYONE. TEACH ME TO WAIT WHEN I'M FEELING IMPATIENT.

GOD'S BETTER IDEA

Better a patient person than a warrior,
one with self-control than one who takes a city.
PROVERBS 16:32 NIV

When you make choices because you feel impatient, you might look like a warrior. Maybe that doesn't sound like a bad thing, but the truth is, when you act out of impatience, you can hurt other people because you insist on getting what you want when you want it.

You could choose self-control instead and wait for God's *better* idea. If you make choices because you feel impatient and then hurt someone, you'll feel bad later. You'll need to apologize and ask that person to forgive you. Of course, the perfect answer is to follow God in the first place. You're not stronger, smarter, or more patient than God. So it makes sense to follow Him and ask Him for help—He will give it.

MAKE ME WISE ENOUGH TO REMEMBER THAT THERE ARE MANY THINGS I DON'T KNOW, FATHER. FEELING IMPATIENT IS A GREAT REMINDER TO PRAY AND TELL YOU WHAT BOTHERS ME AND ASK YOU FOR HELP.

POOR CHOICES

The people became irritable and cross as they traveled. They spoke out against God and Moses: "Why did you drag us out of Egypt to die in this godforsaken country? No decent food; no water."
NUMBERS 21:4–5 MSG

The Bible tells the story of people who were slaves for a very long time. A man named Moses was used by God to rescue the people so they could be free. But they didn't *feel* free. Instead, the people felt impatient. They felt worried. They felt frustrated. These feelings caused them to tell Moses that things were better when they were slaves.

God knows it's easy to feel impatient, but He didn't want these people making poor choices. Feeling impatient led them to complain. They refused to trust God and wouldn't ask for His help. They seemed to think God didn't know what He was doing, and they weren't sure they should have followed God or their leader, Moses.

The people in your life will sometimes make choices you don't like—they might even make the wrong choices. Try hard not to be impatient with them. Show them God's love and grace.

I DON'T NEED THE FEELING OF IMPATIENCE, LORD. TEACH ME TO ALWAYS SHOW YOUR LOVE AND GRACE TO OTHERS.

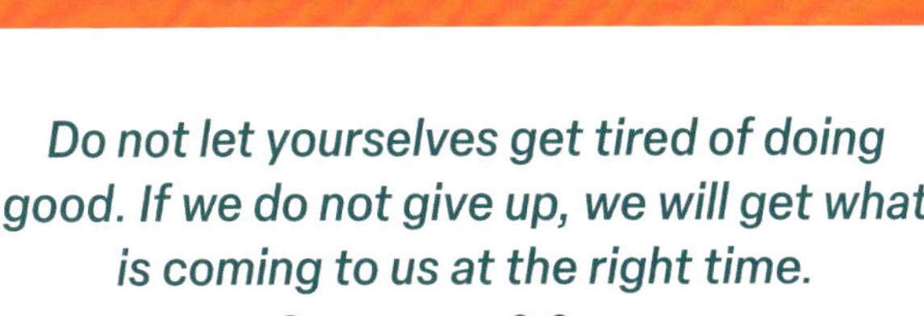

DON'T GiVe UP

Do not let yourselves get tired of doing good. If we do not give up, we will get what is coming to us at the right time.
GALATIANS 6:9 NLV

When you feel impatient, you might choose to give up. You might get tired of doing the right things for the right reasons. God asks you to do everything you can to stay away from the feeling of impatience. Do good things because you follow God—even when you think something is unfair or too hard.

Impatience will lead you to compare how hard things seem for you and how easy things seem for other people. This kind of comparison can cause feelings of jealousy, anger, and frustration. God promises to help, but He never said things would be easy. Don't give up—there's more to your story.

WHEN THINGS SEEM HARD, GOD, I DON'T WANT TO COMPARE MYSELF WITH OTHERS AND THINK THAT YOU TREAT THEM BETTER THAN YOU TREAT ME. IMPATIENCE WILL DO THAT—AND YOU DON'T WANT ME TO FEEL IMPATIENT.

A VERY GOOD CHOICE

I waited patiently for the LORD to help me, and he turned to me and heard my cry.
PSALM 40:1 NLT

When you feel patient, you can be calm because you believe there will be a very good ending to whatever you're struggling with. Everyone struggles, but not everyone makes good choices when they face trouble. King David wrote that he did the hard thing of being patient when he faced difficulties. Because he was patient, David got what he really needed—a God who listened to him. And God didn't just listen to David. . .He helped him.

You might wonder if God listens to you. If you're patient enough to wait for His best answer, then His help will arrive at just the right time.

Being patient is more than a feeling—it's a very wise choice.

WHEN I WANT TO DO ANYTHING BESIDES WAITING, REMIND ME OF DAVID, FATHER. IF A KING KNEW HE NEEDED TO TALK TO YOU FIRST, THEN I WANT TO DO WHAT HE DID. PLEASE LISTEN WHEN I HURT—AND HELP ME.

BEING PATIENT IS MORE
THAN A FEELING—
IT'S A VERY WISE CHOICE.

GOING THE WRONG WAY?

Be happy in your hope. Do not give up when trouble comes. Do not let anything stop you from praying.
ROMANS 12:12 NLV

There are a lot of good things to remember in today's verse. Feel happy because you trust God. Feel patient on hard days. Feel adventurous by making the choice to follow a good God—even when you don't feel like it. There will be days when you feel like doing only what *you* want. God knows this can lead you the wrong way, which is why He wants you to remember that feelings don't always tell you the truth. All feelings—good and bad—can lead you the wrong way. So when your feelings take over, it's a great time to talk to God and ask for His thoughts.

Choose hope even when you don't feel happy. Be patient even when it would be easier to feel angry. Pray even when you're not sure you want to.

WOULD YOU LEAD ME, GOD? I DON'T ALWAYS KNOW WHERE I'M GOING, AND I DON'T KNOW HOW TO GET WHERE YOU WANT ME TO BE. HELP ME TRUST YOU MORE THAN I TRUST MY FEELINGS.

BRAVE AND PATIENT

Be patient. . . . Stay steady and strong.
The Master could arrive at any time.
JAMES 5:8 MSG

Jesus lived with people here on earth. It all started with the Christmas story and continued through Easter—when Jesus died and rose again. He said that someday He would return to earth, and people have been waiting ever since He made that promise. James was one of Jesus' brothers, and he wrote that Jesus would come back, hoping to encourage Jesus' followers to feel brave and patient.

Just because you've never seen Jesus with your own eyes doesn't mean that you won't. You might choose to believe that Jesus will never come back, but that will change the choices you make. Any choices you made *before* you believed Jesus was coming back probably weren't very good choices. Know you can trust what Jesus said. If He said He would. . .He will!

Choose to feel the wonder of all the promises God will keep. And choose patience.

WHEN I'M NOT PATIENT AND WON'T WAIT FOR YOU, THEN I STOP TRUSTING YOU, FATHER. I'LL NEVER BE BETTER OFF BY DOUBTING THAT YOU KEEP YOUR PROMISES. HELP ME TO BELIEVE—AND THEN TO WAIT PATIENTLY FOR YOU.

IT'S A STRUGGLE

Jesus said, "Come to me, all of you who are weary and carry heavy burdens, and I will give you rest."
MATTHEW 11:28 NLT

Do you remember diving underwater for the first time? Going underwater can be scary. Your body is used to breathing. Swimming makes normal breathing impossible. This is kind of what it's like to feel overwhelmed. You have *so* many things to take care of—too many things to think about. Your mind may just want to give up thinking about so much. It's like when your lungs are underwater—it's a struggle.

Jesus talked to a lot of people when He lived on earth. He met people who were overwhelmed. They just wanted to give up. But He had better advice: When you're very tired and life is just too hard—*pray* and tell God all about how you feel and the difficult things you face. The best news is what Jesus promised next: "I will give you rest."

TROUBLE CAN MAKE THINGS SEEM TOO HARD, LORD. THERE ARE SO MANY CHOICES, AND I DON'T HAVE ALL THE ANSWERS. BUT YOU DO. I CAN GET VERY TIRED ON THE HARD DAYS. PLEASE HELP ME.

A LIFE RING

Do not worry. Learn to pray about everything.
Give thanks to God as you ask Him for what you need.
PHILIPPIANS 4:6 NLV

When bad things happen, it can seem like they invite other bad things to join the party. It's common to feel overwhelmed when there's more bad than good and more hard than easy moments. You just can't deal with everything that competes for your attention. It can feel like you're in a flood and need a life ring so you can be rescued.

God wants you to know there's nothing—*nothing*—that you can't pray about. There's nothing—*nothing*—worth worrying about. You never have to feel overwhelmed and face a struggle all by yourself. In fact, knowing that you are never alone should mean that you tell God, "Thank You!" before you even receive His rescue.

Feeling overwhelmed? It's time to trust God.

WHEN I FEEL OVERWHELMED, I DON'T NEED TO KEEP FEELING THAT WAY, GOD. REMIND ME TO TALK TO YOU ABOUT MY FEELINGS SO YOU CAN SHOW ME THE TRUTH THAT CAN CHANGE THE WAY I FEEL.

HE KNOWS EVERYTHING

My flesh and my heart may fail,
but God is the strength of my heart.
PSALM 73:26 NIV

Your body and mind are limited in what they can do. You can't run for a week without stopping. You can't stop eating for a year. You can't know everything there is to know even if you agree to study every moment of your life. But God doesn't have those kinds of limits. He never gets tired, doesn't need food, and already knows everything.

Your body and mind prove that they can't do everything, but that's just a reminder that God is the one who can give you strength when you feel overwhelmed.

God isn't saying that you shouldn't try to be strong. But He is saying that you shouldn't try to do anything *alone*. You'll need God as a friend who is stronger and wiser than anyone or anything else. He can help. He *will* help. Have you asked Him?

SOMETIMES THE THOUGHTS I THINK AREN'T HELPFUL, FATHER. SOMETIMES I JUST CAN'T DO ALL THE THINGS I THINK I SHOULD DO. WHEN I FEEL OVERWHELMED, HELP ME REMEMBER THAT YOU NEVER FEEL THAT WAY.

AFTER TRYING, TRUST

We don't want you in the dark, friends, about how hard it was. . . . It was so bad we didn't think we were going to make it. We felt like. . .it was all over for us. As it turned out, it was the best thing that could have happened. Instead of trusting in our own strength or wits to get out of it, we were forced to trust God totally.

2 CORINTHIANS 1:8–9 MSG

Life was hard for the apostle Paul. Things didn't look very promising. Paul tried everything possible to survive, but he wasn't starring in a reality TV show. He didn't have to outlast anyone else before asking God for help. So Paul made the good choice to trust God.

It's silly to wait to call on God when you feel overwhelmed. There may be times when you're overwhelmed and left with only one choice—a choice you should have made much earlier. When all else fails, trust God. Before doing the same old things that have *never* worked, trust God.

I DON'T WANT TO HAVE TO BE FORCED TO TRUST YOU, LORD. PLEASE HELP ME CHOOSE TRUST BEFORE IT'S THE LAST POSSIBLE CHOICE I CAN MAKE.

UNDERSTAND OTHERS

Those who trust in the LORD will find new strength. They will soar high on wings like eagles. They will run and not grow weary. They will walk and not faint.

ISAIAH 40:31 NLT

If feelings don't always tell the truth, then why pay any attention to them? For starters, they help you understand the world around you. They help you learn how you respond to overwhelming situations. Maybe one of the best reasons for feelings is that they help you understand how other people feel when they struggle. Knowing more about feelings will help you be a better friend.

When you're confused about how you feel, trust God. He'll give unexpected strength that will allow you to walk, run, and fly in the direction He would like you to go. You'll meet people who have feelings just like you do. They'll appreciate knowing that you understand how they feel. And you can encourage them by showing them that God can help them when they're struggling with their feelings.

FEELINGS ARE IMPORTANT, LORD GOD. HELP ME USE MY FEELINGS TO UNDERSTAND OTHERS AND THE WORLD AROUND ME.

Freedom Focus

The heart is free where the Spirit of the Lord is. The Lord is the Spirit.
2 CORINTHIANS 3:17 NLV

Did you know you can *be* free but not *feel* free? When you feel overwhelmed, you probably don't feel free. It can feel like someone has wrapped their arms around you and won't let go. Sometimes you feel trapped.

It may be hard to understand, but freedom is a gift God gives to people who need to learn what freedom feels like. You see, some people think freedom is being able to do whatever they want, whenever they want. But true freedom is more like this: When you follow God, you have the freedom to do right things, good things, and helpful things. Feel free to walk with God, talk with God, and do things for and with God. The freedom you have is in doing great things with God, and there are no limitations. Your heart is free to follow God. *Go with Him.*

HELP ME UNDERSTAND FREEDOM, FATHER. I WANT TO WALK WITH YOU, KNOWING THERE ARE NO RESTRICTIONS THAT STOP ME FROM DOING THE GOOD THINGS YOU WANT ME TO DO.

Everyone should be quick to listen, slow to speak and slow to become angry.

SPLINTERS AND PEBBLES

*Everyone should be quick to listen,
slow to speak and slow to become angry.*
JAMES 1:19 NIV

You've been annoyed before, haven't you? Feeling annoyed is like having a splinter under your skin or a pebble in your shoe. You can't seem to get rid of the constant irritation. It makes you feel uncomfortable and unhappy.

People might say things to you that feel like splinters or pebbles, and you get annoyed. God gave us a good way to tell that annoyed feeling to go away: First, stop arguing and pay attention to what's happening. And then be sure to listen well and speak only after you've thought about your words.

If you spend too much time feeling annoyed, you might get angry—and anger is an emotion that's hard to stop before it causes a lot of damage.

Sometimes when you let bad feelings stay in your thoughts too long, even worse feelings show up. Listen more. . .then carefully consider what you're going to say *before* you speak.

SOMETIMES I GET ANNOYED BY THINGS LIKE SPLINTERS, PEBBLES, AND PEOPLE, GOD. HELP ME REMEMBER THAT THE THINGS THAT ANNOY ME AREN'T WORTH GETTING ANGRY ABOUT.

Be Bold, Be Confident, Feel Free

Through faith in [Jesus] we may approach God with freedom and confidence.
EPHESIANS 3:12 NIV

Because freedom is an opportunity to do something amazing with God's help, then you should always feel free to get closer to Him. You can get close to Him by doing what He wants you to do—by obeying Him. You can get close by talking to Him in prayer. Be bold. Be confident. Feel free.

When you feel this kind of *free*, you can always get the answers you need to questions about life. After all, if you can be close to God, then you don't have to just guess what He wants you to do, because God wants to—and will—teach you. He wants you to know the truth, and He will guide you into truth as you trust Him and believe in Him. This kind of freedom means you're beginning to understand that the plan God has for your life is amazing, and you want to do all the good things He already knows you can—*with His help*.

MAKE ME CURIOUS ENOUGH TO THINK, LORD. MAKE ME BOLD ENOUGH TO ASK QUESTIONS. MAKE ME WISE ENOUGH TO WALK WITH YOU ANYWHERE YOU WANT ME TO GO.

IT JUST GETS BETTER

I don't think there's any comparison between the present hard times and the coming good times.
ROMANS 8:18 MSG

You already know that you can feel overwhelmed when life is hard. It can seem like the most difficult time ever. You don't feel free. You don't feel happy. You don't even feel thankful. You just want a better day with fewer problems.

God said that this day *will* come. One day, when you're with God in heaven, the hard days you experienced here on earth won't seem so bad. Why? Because the good times God promised will have arrived—and they won't ever end.

When you let Jesus rescue you, the freedom you feel is true freedom even when hard days show up and stay far too long. The freedom God gives never takes a break, and when the good times God promises have started, they'll just get better and better.

I DON'T LIKE BAD TIMES, GOD, BUT YOU KNOW THAT. I WANT GOOD TIMES, OR AT LEAST BETTER TIMES. HELP ME FEEL THE FREEDOM OF KNOWING THAT I'LL GET TO LIVE WITH YOU FOREVER SOMEDAY.

MERCY AND GRACE

Now there is no condemnation for those who belong to Christ Jesus. And because you belong to him, the power of the life-giving Spirit has freed you from the power of sin.

ROMANS 8:1–2 NLT

You're free because God created you for freedom—even if you don't feel it. It's a good idea to remember this good news. Before Jesus rescued you from sin, your bad choices were like a chain around your neck. You couldn't seem to get too far from sin before you broke another one of God's rules. Maybe you wanted to do better, but it was so hard to make the right choices.

When God rescues a boy like you, He offers freedom to stop chasing things that encourage you to break His rules. He breaks the chains that keep you close to sin. His power changes your choices. When you belong to Jesus because you've allowed Him to rescue you, He forgives you instead of condemning you. He shows mercy and grace. *You need both.*

I DON'T WANT SIN TO CONTROL ME, FATHER. HELP ME RECOGNIZE THAT THE ONLY REAL FREEDOM I HAVE IS THE FREEDOM YOU GIVE ME.

Please God and Live Free

Christian brother, you were chosen to be free. Be careful that you do not please your old selves by sinning because you are free. Live this free life by loving and helping others.
GALATIANS 5:13 NLV

Did you know that when you break God's rules, you're saying that you don't like being free? It might even seem like you're perfectly okay with doing what God's enemy wants you to do. But remember that God's enemy can't rescue you. He likes to see you make bad choices and then remind you that you'll always make mistakes.

But that's not what God does. He helps you feel free by showing you how to live free. The way to live free is by doing everything you can to please God—not His enemy.

When you break God's rules, you feel bad, don't you? God wants you to experience freedom instead. This free feeling gets even stronger when you love others and help them when they need it.

I NEED TO THINK OF FEELING FREE IN A NEW WAY, LORD. IT'S BIGGER THAN DOING WHAT I WANT. HELP ME DO WHAT YOU WANT TODAY AND EVERY DAY.

LIFT OTHERS UP

Do everything without complaining and arguing, so that no one can criticize you. Live clean, innocent lives as children of God, shining like bright lights.
PHILIPPIANS 2:14–15 NLT

The words you speak can get you into trouble when you're feeling annoyed. It might be easy to tell other people exactly why they annoy you, and you might even feel better after telling them—for a little while anyway. You might come away from your outburst feeling like you didn't get it right. You may have hurt someone who didn't even know they'd done anything wrong. You might even wish you had taken time to let the feeling of calm take over before opening your mouth.

It's easy to complain and argue, but when we do, it usually makes others not want to get too close to us. If you talk about how much people annoy you, others may think it won't be long before you're annoyed with them too. They might not want to be your friend. Be a light that shines on the good things God is teaching you. Spend less time talking about the people who irritate you and more time lifting others up.

YOU'RE A FRIEND I CAN TRUST, LORD.
HELP ME BE A FRIEND OTHERS CAN TRUST.

TRUST GOD, FORGIVE OTHERS

I pray that God's great power will make you strong, and that you will have joy as you wait and do not give up.
COLOSSIANS 1:11 NLV

When you're annoyed, you become irritable, impatient, and angry. Being annoyed and not dealing with your feelings can leave you unhappy and wanting to see others punished for making you feel bad. God wants you to know that your feelings are important—He really does care. However, He also wants you to *pause* before you respond. God doesn't want you to give up or give in to bad feelings that aren't helpful.

So, what should you do? Talk to an adult you trust. They can help you separate your annoyed feelings from your actions. . .and help you make good choices.

God wants you to know that that the feeling of being annoyed won't last forever. He wants you to know that the consequences of the choices you make when you're annoyed will last much longer than your feelings. So trust God. . .and forgive others.

YOU COULD GET ANNOYED WITH ME, GOD. AFTER ALL, I DON'T ALWAYS MAKE GOOD DECISIONS. I'M GLAD YOU FORGIVE. I'M GLAD YOU WAIT. I'M GLAD YOU NEVER GIVE UP ON ME.

VERY GOOD GIFTS

Godliness with contentment is great gain. For we brought nothing into the world, and we can take nothing out of it. But if we have food and clothing, we will be content with that.
1 TIMOTHY 6:6–8 NIV

The opposite of feeling annoyed is being satisfied. This is when you're content with what you have and can't think of anything to complain about. When you're satisfied, you don't feel like asking for anything else, and you're happy to follow God. Satisfied is a very good place to be.

Even if you don't have everything you want, you probably have everything you need. God is the one who makes sure people have His help. He wants people to feel satisfied with what He offers and blessed when they have what they need.

Everything you have today is more than you were born with—food, clothing, shelter. . . Each of these things came from a person who cared for you as you began to grow up. It makes no sense to feel annoyed when God provides exactly what you need.

BEING SATISFIED AND BEING GRATEFUL ARE WONDERFUL FEELINGS, FATHER. HELP ME UNDERSTAND THAT I WILL ALWAYS HAVE ENOUGH BECAUSE YOU GIVE VERY GOOD GIFTS.

Like Being Home

You're all I want in heaven! You're all I want on earth! . . . I've made Lord GOD my home. God, I'm telling the world what you do!
PSALM 73:25, 28 MSG

It's hard to complain about anything when you feel satisfied. If you tried, it might be like saying, "God, thank You for everything. I have everything I need, but I still don't have *enough*. I want more—and right now would be good." God wants you to talk to Him. When you do, ask Him for the things you need, but remember to thank Him for what He has already given you. Never demand things from God.

You can feel satisfied, thankful, and content knowing that even if God doesn't give you everything you've asked for—your wants—He still gives you what you need. He gives you Himself.

With God, you'll always have everything you need. Being with Him feels like being home. Sharing God's love with others will help them discover how they can feel satisfied too!

YOU'RE ALL I WANT, LORD. HELP ME FEEL SATISFIED. HELP ME TELL EVERYONE I KNOW ABOUT THE GOOD GIFTS YOU KEEP GIVING TO ME.

NOTICE THE GOOD

Be thankful in all circumstances, for this is God's will for you who belong to Christ Jesus.
1 THESSALONIANS 5:18 NLT

It's easy to feel satisfied when everything is going your way. You're happy when good things happen—you get good grades in school, other kids think you're cool, you make the team. . . It's harder to feel satisfied when someone says they don't like you, you struggle with schoolwork, or you receive bad news.

No matter what you're going through, you can be thankful. Even when people and situations seem unfair, you can be thankful because God is more than fair. You don't have to love everything about your life to find something to be thankful for. The problem is that so many people focus only on the good things that *could* happen and overlook the good things God is doing every day—the kind of good things people don't seem to notice.

God wants you to feel thankful and content, and those feelings happen when you simply start to notice the good things. When you take time to see the good, you'll begin to experience gratitude.

I HAVEN'T SAID "THANK YOU" ENOUGH, GOD. HELP ME FEEL THANKFUL BY GETTING MY ATTENTION AND MAKING ME SEE HOW GOOD YOU ARE TO ME.

WHEN YOU TAKE TIME
TO SEE THE GOOD,
YOU'LL BEGIN TO
EXPERIENCE GRATITUDE.

HONOR GOD, HELP OTHERS

*If you eat or drink or whatever you do,
do everything to honor God.*
1 CORINTHIANS 10:31 NLV

To feel satisfied, you can't hang out with selfishness. When you always want more, you'll *never* be satisfied. When you always want something better, you're less thankful than you should be for what you already have. It's important to recognize God's gifts and be thankful.

Think of all the things you can do to start living with a grateful heart today. Look at everything you know how to do—your talents and gifts. These are things to be thankful for, and they're things you can use to show honor and respect to the God who gave you these abilities in the first place. God also wants you to use your skills to help others recognize Him.

Don't keep your talents hidden. Use them to honor God and help others. Be satisfied with these gifts and thank God for them when you pray.

I DON'T WANT TO BE SELFISH, FATHER. REMIND ME TO USE ALL THINGS I KNOW HOW TO DO—AND ALL THE THINGS YOU TEACH ME—TO HONOR YOU AND HELP OTHERS.

NO LONGER GUILTY

If we confess our sins, he is faithful and just and will forgive us our sins and purify us from all unrighteousness.

1 JOHN 1:9 NIV

No one likes to feel guilty, but everyone *is* guilty. God created rules that people are supposed to follow, but every person breaks at least one of His rules. You might feel guilty when you understand that you did something God said you shouldn't do. While guilt isn't a fun feeling, it's a useful feeling. Why? Because it helps you remember to get close to God, learn from Him, and receive His help.

The good news is that God doesn't want you to feel guilty all the time. He forgives. And when He does, that means you're no longer guilty.

Some people spend a very long time stuck in guilt. Feeling guilty means you agree there are rules and they should be followed—and you feel very bad about breaking those rules. The good news is that when you feel guilty, you can admit you were wrong and leave that guilty feeling behind.

FEELING GUILTY MAKES ME SAD, LORD. I WANT TO DO THE RIGHT THING, BUT SOMETIMES I DON'T. I HAVE BEEN WRONG, AND I NEED TO BE FORGIVEN. I NEED TO FEEL FORGIVEN.

A KING IS FORGIVEN

Wash me clean from my guilt. Purify me from my sin. For I recognize my rebellion.
PSALM 51:2–3 NLT

King David broke God's rules and felt very guilty. He couldn't undo what he did, but he could admit he was guilty. He could ask God for help. He could be forgiven. So he admitted he was wrong and asked God for help. King David was forgiven.

A long-lasting feeling of guilt wouldn't have helped the king. He must have remembered a time when he hadn't sinned and was innocent and clean. King David remembered that he could feel that way again—but not with the feeling of guilt in his heart. He had to get rid of that first. The king didn't make excuses. He didn't blame anyone else. David admitted he was wrong, and God forgave him. God made the king innocent again and gave him the chance to experience new, much better feelings.

What David did to get rid of the feeling of guilt is what you need to do too. Admit without giving excuses. And then? Feel forgiven.

IT'S EASY TO BLAME OTHER PEOPLE FOR THE BAD CHOICES I MAKE, FATHER. WHEN I FEEL GUILTY, HELP ME ADMIT WHAT I DID WRONG AND THEN ACCEPT YOUR FORGIVENESS.

GOD'S RULES

If you obey all the Laws but one, you are as guilty as the one who has broken them all.
JAMES 2:10 NLV

Did you know that it's possible to *be* guilty but not *feel* guilty? This happens when people don't believe they need to follow God's rules. They choose to do what they want without worrying about what God thinks. But since God made everything and also made the rules, what He says is more important than what anyone else thinks.

This is another example of how the way you feel can be wrong. Because there are rules that God created, breaking one of them means you're guilty and need to be forgiven. Even if you don't want to believe it, it's still true.

The good news is that forgiveness is possible. You can stop feeling guilty because you *do* believe and you're willing to admit that you were wrong to break God's rules.

I WANT MY FEELINGS TO HELP ME DISCOVER TRUTH, LORD. IF I BREAK EVEN ONE OF YOUR RULES, MAY MY GUILTY FEELINGS HELP ME TO SAY "I'M SORRY."

PROVEN INNOCENT

[God] will make your righteous reward shine like the dawn, your vindication like the noonday sun.
PSALM 37:6 NIV

The feeling of innocence is something people like more than the feeling of guilt. When you know the right thing to do and then *do* the right thing, you can feel pretty good about it.

There might be people who think you haven't done the right thing, but there is a word in Psalm 37:6 that clears it all up: That word is *vindication*, and it means you're proven innocent to people who thought you were wrong.

Job was a man in the Bible who was innocent, but his friends kept telling him why they thought he was guilty and why he should feel guilty. By the end of his story, his innocence was proven to be true. God knows whether you're innocent or not. He can be trusted when people struggle to believe the truth.

I KNOW I'VE BEEN GUILTY OF BREAKING YOUR RULES, GOD. WHEN I'M INNOCENT, YOU CAN HELP OTHERS SEE THE TRUTH.

A Clean Record

Clean the slate, God, so we can start the day fresh! Keep me from stupid sins, from thinking I can take over your work; then I can start this day sun-washed, scrubbed clean of the grime of sin.

PSALM 19:12–13 MSG

You need a fresh start—a second chance. You should want that. And the good news is that God offers it. Ask God to clean your record and start your day as if you'd never made a wrong choice.

Ask God to help you make excellent choices. Ask Him to help you stop thinking you know it all. Remember that God never needs you to take over when He's trying to teach you.

It's a great feeling when God declares you innocent. Of course, every time you break His rules, you'll need to admit your wrongdoing so God can forgive you and declare you innocent once more. Feeling innocent is connected to those times when God scrubs you clean from a nasty splash of sin grime.

I WANT TO BE INNOCENT, FATHER. IF YOU WASH ME CLEAN, THEN I'LL BE CLEAN. WHEN YOU SHOW ME THE WAY, I WANT TO FOLLOW YOUR DIRECTIONS.

WHAT GOD ASKS

Everyone knows that you are obedient to the Lord. This makes me very happy. I want you to be wise in doing right and to stay innocent of any wrong.
ROMANS 16:19 NLT

People who make good, right, and innocent choices should be encouraged. You can make choices that show that you want to honor God and follow His plan for your future.

This kind of living means you need to obey. Maybe that doesn't exactly sound like freedom, but the truth is, you will *always* obey someone. It could be friends who have a list of bad ideas they want you to try. It could be God's greatest enemy, who has never wanted you to do the right thing. Or you could obey God, who always knows best.

Obedience can be as easy as paying attention to the God who wants the best for you. It doesn't make sense to follow someone who seems happy when you make bad choices, does it? If you want to feel innocent, then be innocent. Simply do what God asks.

YOU WANT ME TO FEEL INNOCENT, LORD. HELP ME OBEY YOU AND NOT SOMEONE ELSE WHO DOESN'T REALLY CARE ABOUT ME.

NOT RiGHT!

Giving thanks and speaking bad words come from the same mouth. My Christian brothers, this is not right!
JAMES 3:10 NLV

Some people go to church, sing Christian songs, and hear good words from scripture. But then they go home and don't think much about God until the next weekend. You might believe God is awesome one day but speak bad words about other people the next. God wants you to choose only one way to live—and it doesn't involve speaking bad words. God's Word tells us, "This is not right!"

When you follow Jesus, you'll find that feeling innocent is impossible when you're guilty. If God wants you to be kind in the way you speak to—and about—other people, you can't say, "I love God but not other people."

How will anyone want to know more about Jesus if they see that you don't care about other people or that you say hurtful things about them?

WHAT I SAY AND DO IS IMPORTANT TO HOW I FEEL, GOD. I NEED TO BE CAREFUL IN WHAT I THINK, SAY, AND DO. HELP ME TO BE INNOCENT AND MAKE GOOD CHOICES THAT PLEASE YOU.

Above all, clothe yourselves with love, which binds us all together in perfect harmony.

GOD'S MOST IMPORTANT RULE

Above all, clothe yourselves with love, which binds us all together in perfect harmony.
COLOSSIANS 3:14 NLT

Because you have a choice, always choose love. *Never choose hate.* Don't even say, "I don't care." Wear love like your favorite hoodie. Keep it with you always. It will attract people to you and can even turn people who don't like you into true friends.

Jesus said there are two rules that are greater than the rest: Those rules are to love God and then love everyone else. Maybe the reason these rules are most important is that when you love God, you choose to follow Him. When you love people, you show them that there's a better way to live. You don't need to feel jealous, angry, or rude. You can care about other people even when they disagree with you. Sometimes people forget that.

No wonder God said love was His most important rule!

HELP ME TO FOLLOW YOUR GREAT RULES, FATHER. EVEN WHEN I DON'T FEEL LOVING, HELP ME DO THINGS THAT SHOW LOVE SO OTHERS CAN SEE YOU IN ME.

DO YOU KNOW WHAT I HATE?

Let those who love the LORD hate evil, for he guards the lives of his faithful ones and delivers them from the hand of the wicked.
PSALM 97:10 NIV

Did you know that God said it was okay to feel hatred? No, He doesn't want you to hate people or His creation. *He wants you to hate the idea of evil.* Wrong choices lead you to guilt, which can also lead you to forgiveness. But first you must love God and hate anything that tries to put distance between you and Him.

You should never run toward something that takes you farther away from God. God hates sin and evil, and He wants you to feel the same way. One reason you might hate evil is that it always hurts people. That includes people you know and love, as well as people you haven't met yet.

Why would you ever love something that God hates?

HELP ME AVOID CHOOSING TO BREAK YOUR RULES, FATHER. I WANT TO HATE SIN BECAUSE YOU HATE SIN. HELP ME LOVE YOU MORE EVERY SINGLE DAY.

The Never Good Thoughts

[Jesus said,] "If you find the godless world is hating you, remember it got its start hating me."
JOHN 15:18 MSG

When people hate each other, they aren't just saying that they don't like each other—they often try very hard to find ways to hurt each other. If you feel hatred toward someone, you'll think a lot about them, but you won't have good thoughts. You won't want them to succeed. You'll want other people to hate that person. And you'll want bad things to happen to anyone who likes the person you hate.

Sadly, Jesus was familiar with this kind of hatred. He saw so many people do everything they could to hurt Him. And they did hurt Him. . .but they couldn't change the good things He would do for them and for you.

If you feel like someone hates you, just remember that God knows what it's like. He can give you a better set of feelings. Just ask Him.

I DON'T WANT TO HATE PEOPLE, AND I DON'T WANT THEM TO HATE ME, LORD. BUT IF THEY DO, HELP ME REMEMBER THAT YOUR LOVE IS SO MUCH BIGGER AND BETTER THAN ALL THE HATE THAT HAS EVER EXISTED IN THE WHOLE WORLD.

THINGS GOD HATES

There are six things the LORD hates—no, seven things he detests: haughty eyes, a lying tongue, hands that kill the innocent, a heart that plots evil, feet that race to do wrong, a false witness who pours out lies, a person who sows discord in a family.

PROVERBS 6:16–19 NLT

Feeling hatred toward people is never what God wants. But you just read that there are seven *things* God hates. What's the difference? Well, people are made in God's image, and they were created to come close to God. The *things* God hates are things that keep people from looking for Him. When God feels hatred toward these things, He's saying He doesn't want things like pride, lying, and evil to stop you from finding Him.

All these things are choices you can make. While He'll always love *you*, God can hate the choices you make if it means they will get in the way of you spending time with Him.

SINCE YOU HATE PRIDE, LYING, AND EVIL, HELP ME STAY AWAY FROM THEM, GOD. HELP ME FIND WHAT YOU LOVE AND THEN LEARN TO LOVE THOSE THINGS TOO.

GET RID OF HATE

Whoever says he is in the light but hates his brother is still in darkness.
1 JOHN 2:9 NLV

When you say you follow God but you hate some people, then the darkness caused by not truly following God (who is light) will leave you trying to find a good way out of a bad situation. Feeling hatred toward someone *will not* help you know or serve God better. Hating someone will just make life harder because you'll spend so much time thinking about that person and what he may have done to hurt you. Your fixation on this person will cause you to struggle to see God in anything.

If you have chosen to hate but want to be close to God, you'll need to get rid of the feeling of hatred first. God offers a perfect trade-off—love.

Feeling hate means you won't recognize God's light that will help you get to the good place He has for you. Ask God to help you see His light today.

I DON'T KNOW HOW I COULD EVER THINK THAT IT'S POSSIBLE TO LOVE YOU AND YET HATE PEOPLE YOU'VE CREATED, FATHER. I WANT TO CHOOSE TO SEE THE GOOD—THE LIGHT—THAT YOU LONG FOR ME TO SEE.

NO CONFUSION

"No one can serve two masters. Either you will hate the one and love the other, or you will be devoted to the one and despise the other."
MATTHEW 6:24 NIV

Can you follow two different people at the same time? What if they're going different places? What if someone insists you pick only one leader? These are important questions, and the right answer to the first question is *no*. You can't follow (or serve) two different leaders (masters). If you don't agree to walk with God, then you're walking away from Him. If you're asked to pick only one to follow, you need to remember who has actually helped you.

The longer you try to follow God *and* something or someone else, the more you'll side with one and refuse to listen to what the other is saying. God wants you to pick a side—His side—so you're not confused. He certainly doesn't want you to have feelings of hate toward Him.

Because you can't follow two leaders, choose the God who made you, loves you, and has a good plan for you.

FOLLOWING YOU IS THE ADVENTURE OF A LIFETIME, LORD. KEEP ME WALKING IN YOUR DIRECTION. KEEP ME COMPANY.

LOVE. . .AND DON'T STOP

Keep your eyes open, hold tight to your convictions, give it all you've got, be resolute, and love without stopping.

1 CORINTHIANS 16:13–14 MSG

If you're going to run a race, you don't just show up on the day of the race and hope for the best. No, you learn the rules, work to get in shape, and, most importantly, don't quit. You have a finish line waiting for you here in life, so God wants you to keep going.

You might think this sounds like hard work—and it is. But when you pay attention, God always shows you the things you need to know. Believe that running your race is possible because God said it is. Give it all you've got, but remember, this race isn't one you run alone.

Love and don't stop loving. Make the choice to do something that shows love—and soon you'll feel it too. The idea of love is cooperating with God, hanging on when it's hard, and doing your best with His help.

YOU WANT ME TO SHOW LOVE, GOD. THAT'S NOT ALWAYS EASY. HELP ME PAY ATTENTION SO I CAN SEE WHERE YOU WANT ME TO GO NEXT.

WHAT LOVE IS LIKE

We love because he first loved us.
1 JOHN 4:19 NIV

Would you know what love was like if God hadn't shown people what it looked like? God gave good gifts when people complained. He rescued people when they were certain they didn't need it. He offered friendship when people said, "No thanks!"

It's easy for people to try to keep everyone else away. When you don't love or accept the love of others, you may be trying to protect yourself from being hurt. But you never need to worry when it comes to God. He wants a friendship with you, and He gave more than anyone ever has to make that friendship possible. He's just waiting for you to accept His gift.

You can choose to love first and *then* feel it when you come to believe that God loves you. He loved you before you even knew anything about Him. That's true love!

HELP ME FEEL YOUR LOVE, GOD. I WANT TO BE FRIENDS WITH YOU. KNOWING THAT YOU LOVE ME HELPS ME REMEMBER THAT EVERYONE NEEDS LOVE. I WANT TO LOVE OTHERS BECAUSE YOU LOVE ME.

A Different Response

[Jesus said,] "If you love me, show it by doing what I've told you. I will talk to the Father, and he'll provide you another Friend so that you will always have someone with you. This Friend is the Spirit of Truth."
JOHN 14:15–16 MSG

One way God shows how much He loves you is by making sure His Spirit is always with you. John 14 is a great reminder that love is something you *do* first. You can show God that you love Him by learning His Word so you can know—and do—what He asks. This is why love is so important to faith and hope. Love will always change how you think about God. It will also change your willingness to obey Him.

Love—and the feelings that come with it—is part of the way God makes you a new creation. People just respond differently—better—when they're loved.

THANK YOU FOR YOUR SPIRIT. HE TEACHES ME SO MUCH, FATHER. HELP ME TO LEARN GOOD LESSONS AND SHARE THE LOVE YOU GIVE. I LOVE YOU. KEEP CHANGING ME FOR THE BETTER.

When Disappointment Leaves

Hope that is put off makes the heart sick,
but a desire that comes into being is a tree of life.
PROVERBS 13:12 NLV

Birthdays are special days, and many boys like you believe that they'll receive special gifts and a party. But what if your day passes with nothing special? What a disappointment! When you believe and hope for the best, only to be let down, you're left feeling upset.

You've probably had the opposite experience too. Something happens that you've always wished for but never expected would happen. What a great surprise, right? It's a little like finding a bottle of cool water under a shade tree on a very hot day. Unexpected, but so very wonderful!

The reality is that everybody feels disappointed sometimes. But there will also be times when good surprises happen. When you receive something you've hoped for, disappointment has no room to stay.

IT'S NEVER FUN TO FEEL DISAPPOINTED, FATHER. SOMETIMES YOU SEND SURPRISES THAT CHANGE MY DISAPPOINTMENT TO JOY. HELP ME REMEMBER THAT YOU'RE IN CONTROL OF EVERYTHING.

Hope that is put off
makes the heart sick,
but a desire that comes
into being is a tree of life.

Feelings Are Responses

*GOD's name is a place of protection—
good people can run there and be safe.*
PROVERBS 18:10 MSG

Talk to God about your feelings—every single one. If you feel disappointed, you can tell Him. You never need to accuse God of making you feel a certain way. Just tell Him about your emotions and ask Him to help you handle them.

Always remember that the feelings you have may be misleading. Feelings often show how you respond to things that happen. Remember that feelings are responses to things you believe are true, even when they may not be. You might feel disappointed about something until you learn that there's more to the situation than you realized.

Pray and believe that God knows more about your struggles than you do. Respond to disappointment in a healthy way with God's help, and know that it doesn't have to be the only feeling you have in the moment. Ask God to help you understand the situation so you can have the very best response. And it doesn't hurt to remember that God is always, *always* good.

WHEN I FEEL FRUSTRATED AND DISAPPOINTED, GOD, HELP ME LEARN MORE ABOUT WHAT YOU'RE DOING SO I CAN RESPOND (AND FEEL) BETTER.

YOU NEED TO BE RESCUED

The Lord will rescue me. . .and will bring me safely to his heavenly kingdom. To him be glory for ever and ever. Amen.
2 TIMOTHY 4:18 NIV

You may need to be rescued from bad feelings. When you keep bad feelings around for too long, they become more than just a response to unhappy things you've experienced. If bad feelings are encouraged, they can convince you to do things you normally would never do. Feelings can easily fuel your choices.

God can rescue you—*and truly, you need to be rescued.* He can bring you safely away from bad feelings and into His truth. Disappointment and frustration will cause you to have negative thoughts about others that will prevent you from loving them. You might start to think of some people as your enemies. You might even want to treat them badly. In fact, you could begin to believe that your bad response is fair. . .but God can help you recognize that it's not.

God's way is so much better.

MY CHOICES USUALLY LISTEN TO MY FEELINGS, LORD. HELP ME RESPOND TO TROUBLE WITH YOUR TRUTH INSTEAD OF MY EMOTIONS.

GOD PROVIDES

This same God who takes care of me will supply all your needs from his glorious riches, which have been given to us in Christ Jesus.
PHILIPPIANS 4:19 NLT

Adjusting your feelings involves paying less attention to how you feel and more attention to what God says. The apostle Paul is a good example of what this looks like. He had many hard days, and it didn't seem like his situation would get easier. But he didn't blame God. In fact, Paul came alongside other people who struggled and said something like, "God takes care of me, and He will take care of you." This is truth—not feeling.

Paul was able to feel fulfilled (like he had everything he needed) because God decided what was needed, and He made sure Paul had it. Paul was telling the Philippians that God would do the same for them. God would take care of them. God could be trusted. After all, the same God who rescued Paul had a plan for them too. And He has a plan for you!

WHEN WHAT I NEED IS SOMETHING YOU PROVIDE, I'M BLESSED, FATHER. HELP ME REMEMBER THAT I HAVE WHAT I NEED BECAUSE I HAVE YOU.

Seek the God You Need

"The people who do not know God are looking for all these things. Your Father in heaven knows you need all these things. First of all, look for the holy nation of God. Be right with Him. All these other things will be given to you also."
MATTHEW 6:32–33 NLV

When you feel greedy, you want things that God probably doesn't think are important. When you feel this way, you probably aren't wishing for the things God *will* provide. You aren't appreciating the *real needs* that God has already provided for you.

This doesn't mean God doesn't want you to have something you're wishing for, but He knows just what you need and wants to make sure you seek Him for what you need. He also wants you to appreciate what He gives and then share what you have.

God knows what you really need. So do what He asks of you, and He'll be sure to provide for you. Those who follow Him will be thankful for His many blessings every day, and especially thankful in those special times when they receive something they really want.

LET ME FEEL FULFILLED BECAUSE I HAVE WHAT I NEED, GOD. I WILL KEEP LOOKING FOR YOUR LEADING IN EVERY CHOICE I MAKE.

A Mess Gets Help

And me? I'm a mess. I'm nothing and have nothing: make something of me. You can do it; you've got what it takes—but God, don't put it off.
PSALM 40:17 MSG

If you want to feel like you have everything you need, you can start by admitting that without God you're "a mess" who has "nothing." That probably doesn't make you feel very good, but King David knew it was true.

When the king wanted to feel fulfilled, he spoke to God. David believed God could do what he couldn't. David also pleaded with God not to put off helping him.

There's a very good reason to admit that you can't do everything on your own. If you could do everything, would you still need God? You become friends with Him because you need His help. When you come to God, you'll learn so many other reasons to love and follow Him. Depending on Him for help is another way you can feel fulfilled.

I WANT TO GET TO KNOW YOU, LORD. YOU HELP ME. TAKE MY MESS AND SHOW ME A BETTER WAY TO DO WHAT NEEDS TO BE DONE.

COMFORTED AND FULFILLED

The LORD is my shepherd, I lack nothing. He makes me lie down in green pastures, he leads me beside quiet waters, he refreshes my soul. He guides me along the right paths for his name's sake.

PSALM 23:1–3 NIV

Even if you haven't read very much of the Bible before, you've probably heard or read the Twenty-Third Psalm. This psalm is all about how God helps when you face hard days. It's meant to make you feel comforted and protected. God wants you to know your needs are taken care of because He loves and cares about you.

When God is leading you, there's nothing you need that He won't provide. This is a good reminder that God gets to decide what a need really is. If you ask for something that He doesn't believe is a need, you may not receive it. Trust that God knows your needs and will give you everything necessary for your flourishing.

IT'S AN HONOR TO FOLLOW YOU, FATHER. LEAD ME, TEACH ME, AND COMFORT ME. HELP ME REMEMBER THAT WITH YOU, I'M NEVER MISSING OUT ON ANYTHING.

Fear Seeds

"Don't be afraid, for I am with you.
Don't be discouraged, for I am your God.
I will strengthen you and help you. I will hold
you up with my victorious right hand."
ISAIAH 41:10 NLT

A bump in the night, a bully, or even an unexpected quiz can leave you feeling afraid. Sometimes fear can make you think it's a good idea to run away. Fear is a feeling that often refuses to tell you the truth. It lets you think the worst simply because you haven't taken the time to discover the truth.

God said that the feeling of fear isn't necessary when He's with you. You don't need to experience fearful feelings because He's *for* you. He strengthens, helps, and holds you.

Fear is a feeling that easily takes over. Fear grows deep roots and produces very bad fruit. Refuse to plant fear seeds. Fear is a feeling you don't need in your heart.

I WANT TO GET RID OF FEAR SEEDS, GOD. THIS FEELING MAKES ME STRUGGLE TO STAY CALM WHEN BAD THINGS HAPPEN.

CALMER OF THE STORM

At once a bad storm came over the lake. The waves were covering the boat. Jesus was sleeping. His followers went to Him and called, "Help us, Lord, or we will die!" He said to them, "Why are you afraid? You have so little faith!" Then He stood up. He spoke sharp words to the wind and the waves. Then the wind stopped blowing.

MATTHEW 8:24–26 NLV

The Bible tells a story about fear that might help you. Jesus and His disciples were in a boat. Jesus was asleep when a storm came that caused the disciples to be afraid. They were too far from the shore, and they were certain they would die in the storm. They must have tried to do everything they could to deal with the storm, but in their panic, they forgot to ask Jesus for help.

When the men did ask, they were already very afraid. Jesus wondered why. After all, He was with them. If they really trusted Him, then they should have known there was no trouble or storm He couldn't handle.

YOU'RE WITH ME, LORD. I NEED YOU.
KEEP FEAR FAR AWAY FROM ME.

EVEN IF THINGS DON'T WORK OUT PERFECTLY, GOD IS WITH YOU.

THINGS YOU DON'T UNDERSTAND

"Do not be afraid; do not be discouraged, for the LORD your God will be with you wherever you go."

JOSHUA 1:9 NIV

You might feel afraid when you're all alone and something happens that you don't understand. An unexpected knock at the door, someone yelling outside, or the sound of a car coming to a quick stop. Anything you don't expect and don't know how to handle can bring feelings of fear.

That's what happened to the people of Israel. They'd been given a new home in a new land. All they had to do was go into the land and take it. That was something they'd never done before—so they were afraid. Their new leader, Joshua, gave them a message from God: "You do not need to be afraid because I'll be with you."

You need to know that God doesn't want you to be fearful when you experience new things. Even if things don't work out perfectly, God is with you.

HELP ME NOT TO BE AFRAID OF NEW EXPERIENCES, GOD. WHEN YOU WANT ME TO GO, I NEVER NEED TO BE AFRAID.

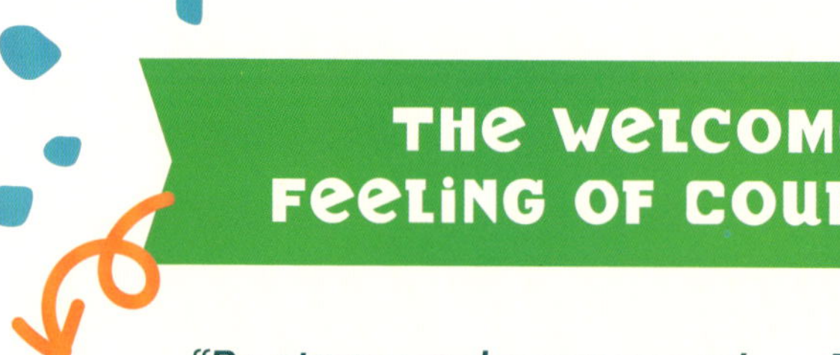

The Welcome Feeling of Courage

"Be strong and courageous! . . . For the LORD your God will personally go ahead of you. He will neither fail you nor abandon you."
DEUTERONOMY 31:6 NLT

Today's verse sounds a lot like yesterday's verse, but this one introduces a new feeling that's the opposite of fear: *courage*. When you're feeling courageous, you're ready to face challenges with God's help. It doesn't mean you won't feel fear, but it does mean you'll trust God so much that you'll feel brave enough to do hard things.

God never fails, so walking with Him offers so much more than when we walk alone. But you always have a choice. You can continue to feel frightened, or you can choose to feel courageous. It all depends on who you trust.

IT'S PRETTY DIFFICULT TO FEEL COURAGEOUS WHEN I'M AFRAID, LORD. GIVE ME THE COURAGE TO DO HARD THINGS WHEN FEAR TELLS ME I CAN'T.

TRUST, SELF-DISCIPLINE, AND COURAGE

Watch and keep awake! Stand true to the Lord. Keep on acting like men and be strong.
1 CORINTHIANS 16:13 NLV

Things happen in life that encourage you to feel all different ways. And if you don't pay attention, you just might live with the wrong feelings. When you pay attention and believe that what God says is true, something amazing happens.

It's a little bit like practicing to get better at any skill. It requires trust, self-discipline, and courage. Follow God with everything you've got, but remember that you're part of a team and He's your coach. He knows how to win, so pay attention to His game plan.

You're growing up and getting stronger. The same needs to be true about your friendship with God. When you make the choice to get closer to Him, you'll discover that your feelings line up with the truth that God wants you to believe.

I NEED TO FEEL COURAGEOUS ENOUGH TO OBEY YOU, FATHER. I NEED TO BELIEVE THAT WHAT YOU SAY IS TRUE AND WORTH PAYING ATTENTION TO. HELP ME GROW UP IN MY FRIENDSHIP WITH YOU.

The Strength You Need

[Jesus said,] "That's my parting gift to you. Peace. I don't leave you the way you're used to being left—feeling abandoned, bereft. So don't be upset. Don't be distraught."
JOHN 14:27 MSG

When you feel afraid, you might think no one cares. When fear has you in its grip, you don't feel peace. When you're scared, you feel upset and worried.

When Jesus was ready to leave earth to return to heaven, He offered a gift—peace. Jesus didn't want His followers to feel abandoned. He also knew that those who followed Him would miss Him. That's why He encouraged them to be courageous and stay away from feelings of fear, terror, or worry.

When you move, join a new club at school, or want to make a new friend, you'll need to feel courage. So many feelings can make you uncertain. But courage brings hope, invites trust, and believes the truth. The real strength you need can always be found in the God you follow.

I NEED TO FEEL COURAGEOUS ENOUGH TO DISCOVER YOUR PEACE, GOD. I CAN DO THIS BY CASTING OFF FEAR AND WORRY. HELP ME REJECT WHAT'S NEVER HELPFUL AND ACCEPT WHAT ONLY YOU CAN GIVE.

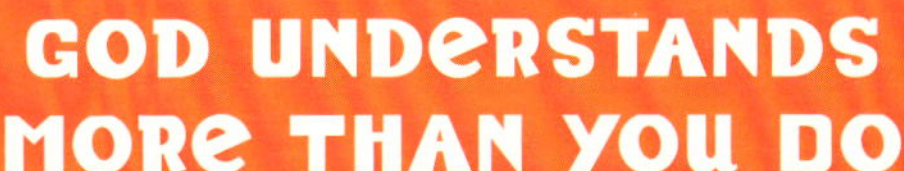

GOD UNDERSTANDS MORE THAN YOU DO

Trust in the LORD with all your heart and lean not on your own understanding; in all your ways submit to him, and he will make your paths straight.
PROVERBS 3:5–6 NIV

You'll need courage to move away from any misleading feelings. The way you "think" things are may not be the way they really are. It's possible to think certain things are true because they "feel" that way. Those kinds of feelings can cause you to make the wrong choices.

Make the courageous choice to trust God. Follow Him, and He'll straighten out your thinking. There will be plenty of times when your feelings get hurt. But because feelings can affect your choices, you'll need to remember that there's always a better way to understand the things that happen around you—with God's help.

Trusting God might seem hard, because your feelings often feel so big and important that they can trick you into believing that they're the truth. You could be right. . .but God understands more than you do. So trust Him.

I CAN MAKE A MISTAKE AND DECIDE THINGS ARE TRUE BECAUSE THEY FEEL TRUE, LORD. GIVE ME THE COURAGE TO CHANGE HOW I FEEL BECAUSE I KNOW THAT WHAT YOU SAY IS TRUE.

GREED GUARDS

Then [Jesus] said, "Beware! Guard against every kind of greed. Life is not measured by how much you own."
LUKE 12:15 NLT

If God doesn't measure life by how much stuff you own, then why do so many people think money is the most important thing they could have? Greed is the feeling you get when you want what other people have. This feeling shows up when you think you need more and more stuff.

The problem with greed is that it doesn't let you feel satisfied with the things you already have. When you get more, you want more. When you get even more, it still isn't enough.

God wants you to take a stand against the feeling of greed, which will leave you unsatisfied no matter how much you have. If you can't get more stuff, then you feel frustrated, angry, and impatient. These feelings are never good, and they can have a negative influence on the way you think about and treat other people.

I WOULD LOVE TO HAVE EVERYTHING I WANT, FATHER. ONLY YOU KNOW WHAT'S HELPFUL. HELP ME NEVER TO FEEL SO GREEDY THAT I MISS OUT ON CHOOSING YOUR WAY.

MONEY CHASERS

The love of money is the beginning of all kinds of sin. Some people have turned from the faith because of their love for money. They have made much pain for themselves because of this.
1 TIMOTHY 6:10 NLV

Some people will always choose things they can buy over gifts that can't be purchased in a store. These priceless gifts include love, joy, peace, friendship, compassion, and kindness. Money can't make you brave (though it could encourage you to be dishonest). Money can convince you to dislike others if they own more than you do. Don't let feelings of greed cause other bad feelings to take over in your heart.

Greed is like drinking water that only makes you thirstier. No matter how much you drink, you're still thirsty for more.

Money itself isn't necessarily bad, but when money is *all* you want, then you begin to break God's rules. Money can't sin, but *you* can sin by chasing money. When people chase money, they forget God.

HELP ME USE MY STRENGTH TO CHASE AFTER YOU, GOD. HELP ME NEVER TO CHOOSE MONEY OVER FRIENDSHIP WITH YOU.

THE THOUGHTS YOU THINK

Set your minds on things above, not on earthly things.
COLOSSIANS 3:2 NIV

What are you thinking about right now? What were you thinking about an hour ago? What do you think about most? Are you proud of what you think about most?

If your thoughts are focused on what's important to God, you probably feel pretty good. But if you think about all the things *you* want, then you're distracted from the things God loves, the things He wants to teach you, and the ways you could be helping others.

If you think about God on purpose, then you also spend time wondering what you can do to please Him more and keep the feeling of greed away. What you think you want isn't nearly as important as what God wants for you. When you think about God's thoughts, then your thoughts will change too—and so will your feelings.

IF SOMETHING ISN'T MINE, THEN I SHOULDN'T TRY TO TAKE IT, FATHER. BUT YOU'VE GIVEN ME TIME, AND I CAN USE IT WISELY. I CAN SPEND THAT TIME WITH YOU.

WHEN YOU THINK ABOUT GOD'S THOUGHTS, THEN YOUR THOUGHTS WILL CHANGE TOO—AND SO WILL YOUR FEELINGS.

GOD JUST GIVES

You must each decide in your heart how much to give. And don't give reluctantly or in response to pressure. "For God loves a person who gives cheerfully."
2 CORINTHIANS 9:7 NLT

When you feel generous, you don't want to be selfish. If you're generous, you're probably paying attention to all the things God has said about love, joy, and peace.

Generosity means you're willing to share and you *want* to share. You can be generous with God, family, friends, and neighbors.

There's no human who will ever be as generous as God. He's a perfect example of giving more than anyone expected and continuing to share even when people don't fully appreciate it.

God doesn't make you fill out an application to receive His goodness—He just gives. Light, air, water, and food are all things God provides for you. Because He gives cheerfully, He loves to see you learning from His example and even having fun being generous.

HELP ME SHARE WITH OTHERS THE SAME WAY YOU SHARE WITH ME, GOD. HELP ME PAY ATTENTION TO NEEDS AND THEN DO WHAT I CAN TO HELP.

GENEROUS POSSIBILITIES

"In every way I showed you that by working hard like this we can help those who are weak. We must remember what the Lord Jesus said, 'We are more happy when we give than when we receive.'"

ACTS 20:35 NLV

You probably look forward to getting gifts on your birthday or at Christmastime. Lots of people look forward to receiving—and even giving—gifts. Your family might want to see your happy reaction to opening a gift they give to you. The feeling of generosity means that people enjoy giving more than getting.

Maybe you didn't know that God said one of the good reasons to work hard is that some of the money you earn can be used to help others. Your hard work and the feeling of generosity that you experience can bring about feelings of happiness in others when you share with them.

Work helps make generosity possible.

WHEN I EARN MONEY, I MIGHT HAVE PLANS TO SPEND IT ON SOMETHING I WANT, LORD. BUT HELP ME FIRST TO THINK OF OTHERS AND WHAT THEY MIGHT NEED. HELP ME TO BE GENEROUS SO MY WORK CAN HELP OTHERS.

BONUS AND BLESSING

"Give away your life; you'll find life given back, but not merely given back—given back with bonus and blessing. Giving, not getting, is the way."
LUKE 6:38 MSG

The feeling of generosity is *not* typical. Why? Because humans are selfish creatures. When you work hard and make money, it might make sense to save it (not a bad idea), spend it on what you want (some people do), or dream of the next big thing you'd like to own (you probably have something in mind).

Generosity takes away from what you've earned or been given and shares it with someone else. Giving things away doesn't help you get what you want, does it? But when you give, God is pleased. And He can give back to you, "with bonus and blessing." This doesn't mean getting back exactly what you gave. What God gives will always be better than you expect, but it may not be money. Sometimes you might just receive the gift of feeling joy from your giving—and that sticks around far longer than any good feeling you get when you receive.

I WANT TO BE GENEROUS, FATHER, NOT JUST BECAUSE YOU CAN PROVIDE A BONUS AND BLESSING BUT BECAUSE THE WAY YOU DO THINGS SHOWS THERE IS A BETTER WAY FOR EVERYONE.

GENEROSITY HAPPENS WHEN. . .

If anyone has material possessions and sees a brother or sister in need but has no pity on them, how can the love of God be in that person?

1 JOHN 3:17 NIV

If you choose to love, you'll also choose to give. Showing generosity helps people recognize God, because giving is what God does. Without the choice to love, you won't feel the need to give even when you know someone could really use a friend.

Generosity happens when you make the choice to love other people first. God wants to love people through you. People often need to see God's love in you before they search for Him. When you choose to love people, your generosity might be so impactful that they come to think of you as an answer to prayer. Because God loves you, you can love others—and the choice to love makes the feeling of generosity flow from your heart.

YOU WANT ME TO BE GENEROUS BECAUSE I CHOOSE TO, GOD. HELP ME CHOOSE LOVE SO I CAN FEEL GENEROUS.

PROVERBS 11:2

*Pride leads to disgrace,
but with humility
comes wisdom.*

EMBARRASSED WITH PURPOSE

Pride leads to disgrace,
but with humility comes wisdom.
PROVERBS 11:2 NLT

You might feel embarrassed when you do something the wrong way, or when someone makes fun of you, or when you break one of God's rules. Feelings lead you to make decisions—some good, some bad. Embarrassment is a feeling you have when you make choices you wish you hadn't. Embarrassment can be bad—but it can be good too.

If you're embarrassed because you broke one of God's rules and suffered some negative consequences, you might become angry and want people to leave you alone. That's not a very good response. Or you might choose to admit you were wrong. That's an excellent response.

So many of the feelings God has given you can be good or bad. This is true because feelings lead to choices that will either honor God or leave you with regret.

Feelings tell you something about yourself, but they will never be more important than God's instructions.

WHEN I FEEL AWKWARD OR EMBARRASSED, HELP ME MAKE GOOD CHOICES, LORD. IF I NEED TO APOLOGIZE, MAKE ME COURAGEOUS ENOUGH TO SAY, "I'M SORRY."

EMBARRASSMENT: A NEW OPPORTUNITY

None of us is perfectly qualified. We get it wrong nearly every time we open our mouths. If you could find someone whose speech was perfectly true, you'd have a perfect person, in perfect control of life.

JAMES 3:2 MSG

God doesn't ask you to know everything before you follow Him. No human has ever known enough to be perfectly qualified. You've had times when you said something that came out wrong—or you said something that hurt someone else.

You could spend the rest of your life trying to find a person who's perfect, but you won't succeed. It would be a complete waste of time. Instead, you could be paying attention to the already perfect God.

When you feel embarrassed, it isn't because God *wants* you to feel that way. If you feel awkward because someone is better at something than you are, pride might be the problem. Whenever you think you know more than God and are proven wrong, your pride might be hurt a little, but the embarrassment can become a new opportunity to obey Him.

WHEN I FEEL EMBARRASSED, HELP ME UNDERSTAND WHY. THEN I CAN MAKE A CHOICE THAT PLEASES YOU, GOD.

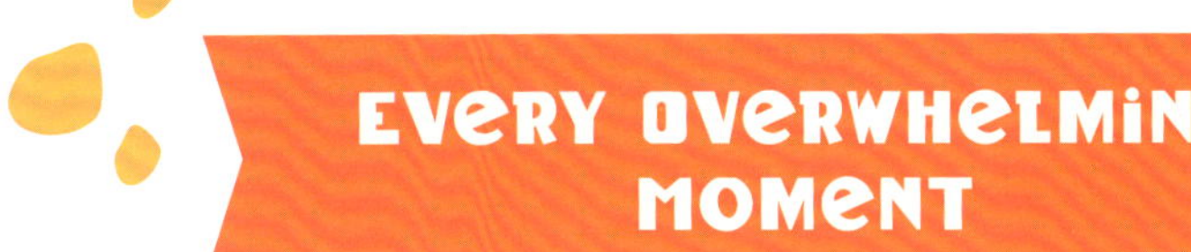

EVERY OVERWHELMING MOMENT

We are hard pressed on every side, but not crushed; perplexed, but not in despair; persecuted, but not abandoned; struck down, but not destroyed.

2 CORINTHIANS 4:8–9 NIV

Everyone will experience times when nothing seems to be going right. You might feel pressured, uncertain, and confused. Or you might feel lost, alone, and hopeless. No one wants to feel these kinds of things. Most people try to avoid these feelings because they can lead to despair.

You may remember reading about how God said trouble would find you even when you weren't looking for it. That's what 2 Corinthians 4 is talking about—overwhelming and very bad days. Pay attention to the last three words in today's verse (if you can't remember what they are, look again). No matter what you experience and no matter how stressful things seem, God reminds you that trouble doesn't mean destruction. He's with you in *every* moment.

WHEN TROUBLE FINDS ME, PLEASE HELP ME, LORD. I DON'T WANT TO FACE OVERWHELMING MOMENTS WITHOUT YOU.

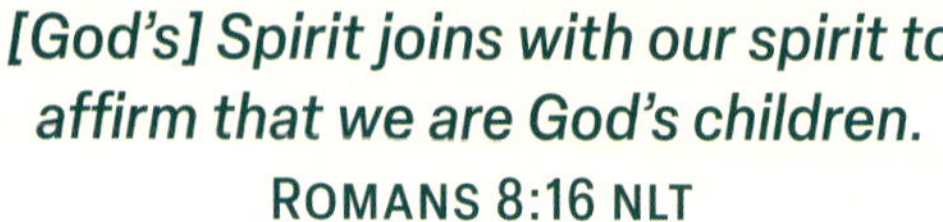

ABSOLUTELY CERTAIN

[God's] Spirit joins with our spirit to affirm that we are God's children.
ROMANS 8:16 NLT

Having a sense of assurance and certainty can be a wonderful feeling. But what exactly are you certain will happen? An A+ on your next test? What you'll have for breakfast six weeks from now? How tall you'll be when you grow up? No one can be 100 percent sure they know the answer to any of these questions.

God says there's one thing you can be certain is true, though—you can be sure He loves you and accepts you as a member of His family. Some people will try to tell you that you can't be certain this is true. But you have a choice to believe people who don't know everything or a God who does know everything.

It's a very good feeling to know for certain that you're loved. It's amazing to be sure that God wants you to be part of His family.

SOMETIMES I FORGET THAT I CAN BE CERTAIN OF YOU, FATHER. HELP ME BELIEVE THE TRUTH THAT YOU LOVE ME SO I CAN ENJOY THE FEELING OF KNOWING I'M PART OF YOUR FAMILY.

GOD-STRENGTH BUBBLE WRAP

I am not ashamed. I know the One in Whom I have put my trust. I am sure He is able to keep safe that which I have trusted to Him until the day He comes again.

2 TIMOTHY 1:12 NLV

You never have to feel ashamed, because you have every reason to trust the heavenly Father. You can feel certain of one very specific thing—everything you trust God to take care of is placed in God-strength Bubble Wrap. Maybe a better way to say this is that the things you believe God will take care of, He will. They will be protected and kept safe.

When Jesus comes again, your trust in God will prove that your certainty in Him was absolutely the right choice to make. God doesn't take your trust and throw it in the trash when you aren't looking. If you trust Him to do what you can't, then you can be certain that He *has*, He *is*, and He *will*.

I HAVE A LOT OF CONCERNS, BUT I TRUST YOU, GOD. MY FUTURE IS SOMETHING YOU WILL TAKE CARE OF. I GIVE ALL MY HOPES TO YOU. YOU'RE SUCH A GOOD FATHER.

BUT WHAT IF IT'S NOT?

Even when the way goes through Death Valley, I'm not afraid when you walk at my side. Your trusty shepherd's crook makes me feel secure.

PSALM 23:4 MSG

Fear makes it hard to know that you're going to be okay. Sometimes, to experience a better feeling, you first need to get rid of the bad feelings that are so demanding.

You want to feel certain that God is on your side, but fear keeps asking one question: "But what if He's not?"

King David wrote about the need to feel certain, but fear kept pushing him around, telling him how to feel. God was leading, but fear kept saying, "But what if He's not?"

That's when David wrote about a place called "Death Valley." This was where fear gathered and tried to influence everyone. The king wisely said that when God walked with him, fear seemed far less intimidating. Is this something you need to remember?

WHEN YOU SAY YOU'RE GOOD, LORD, HELP ME STOP ASKING, "BUT WHAT IF YOU'RE NOT?" I WANT TO BELIEVE. I NEED TO BELIEVE. I NEED TO BE CERTAIN THAT YOU'RE AMAZING.

GOOD PROMISES

I write these things to you who believe in the name of the Son of God so that you may know that you have eternal life.

1 JOHN 5:13 NIV

You can feel certain because God said *He* is certain: He loves you, and the future is His to promise. Feeling assured means you never have to worry. There's no reason to be concerned or to distrust God's promise of rescue. Believe God and know that what He said is absolutely true.

This is different from the way you might experience human promises. Sometimes a person promises something but then doesn't keep their promise. Humans break promises for a lot of different reasons, but when God says He'll do something, you can believe He'll do it. He has *never* broken a promise. He has *never* said something that was untrue. He said He loves you and has plans for your future. This is impressive news from a great God who makes (and keeps) excellent promises.

I HAVE A FUTURE BECAUSE OF YOU, FATHER. THANK YOU FOR YOUR PROMISES. HELP ME BELIEVE THEM AND TRUST YOU WITH EVERYTHING.

Keep the Temperature on Low

He who is slow to get angry has great understanding, but he who has a quick temper makes his foolish way look right.
PROVERBS 14:29 NLV

On the kitchen stove there's a knob or button that adjusts the heat for cooking your food. The higher the number, the hotter it gets. A lower number means less heat. And when you don't want any more heat, you turn the knob or push the button to turn it off.

The feeling of anger has settings like this. When you're introduced to rage in tense moments, you may be tempted to turn your emotional response to the hottest temperature. But the hotter the heat, the easier it is to boil over and spill rage onto everyone around you.

When you feel anger, keep the temperature on low. Even better, turn the heat off completely. God can teach you how to do that. It's never foolish to turn down the heat of rage.

I DON'T WANT TO LET FEELINGS OF RAGE GET HOT, LORD. GIVE ME WISDOM TO CONTROL THIS FEELING BY MAKING CHOICES THAT TURN DOWN THE HEAT.

He who is slow to get angry has great understanding, but he who has a quick temper makes his foolish way look right.

DROP THE BOOMERANG AND BACK AWAY

Don't be quick to fly off the handle. Anger boomerangs. You can spot a fool by the lumps on his head.
ECCLESIASTES 7:9 MSG

The boomerang is something that comes to mind when people talk about the dangers of cause and effect. When you throw a boomerang, it flies away from you, moves in a circle, and then comes back to you. You might catch it, or you could stop paying attention and perhaps get hit by the boomerang.

The Bible describes the feeling of rage as being like a boomerang. It's easy to throw it out there and forget it. But when you do, your rage can return to you. When you feel upset with others, then you can also expect others to feel upset with you.

Rage isn't always a wrong feeling, but God wants you to be careful. . .because once you feel it, it's a feeling that can hang around for a while. It affects you and the people around you.

WHEN I FEEL RAGE, REMIND ME TO PAUSE, FATHER. I DON'T WANT TO HURT OTHERS, AND I DON'T WANT TO GET HURT. KEEP RAGE FROM CAUSING ME BOOMERANG PAIN.

DO SOMETHING ABOUT IT

Refrain from anger and turn from wrath;
do not fret—it leads only to evil.
PSALM 37:8 NIV

Anger shouldn't be a security blanket. Rage doesn't need to be the first thing you choose when someone is rude or angry with you. Rage tells the lie that it's not a good idea to love others. Rage doesn't make room for feelings of peace or joy. Rage leaves you feeling weary and broken. If you hang out with it for long, you'll get hurt. You might even hurt others.

God said that rage can lead to evil (choices that break God's rules and hurt people). But it's a normal feeling. Does this mean you're never supposed to get mad? No. What it means is that when you have feelings of anger, you can do something about it. Rage is a feeling that's calmed by a better choice. Think about how God wants you to respond to other people. Since rage isn't one of His good responses, it's time to respond a different way—His way.

RAGE CAN TELL ME SOMETHING IS WRONG, GOD. HELP ME GIVE YOU WHAT'S WRONG SO YOU CAN DEAL WITH IT AND HELP MAKE IT RIGHT.

The Storm Grew Calm

He calmed the storm to a whisper and stilled the waves. What a blessing was that stillness!
Psalm 107:29–30 NLT

Some people believe this psalm was about the deliverance of the Jewish people from slavery.

We don't know for sure if King David witnessed the calming of an actual storm or experienced God calming the storm of rage inside and replacing it with a feeling of peace.

God had changed the circumstances of the people and brought an unexpected calm in place of the worry, rage, and despair they'd felt. Whatever happened must have had a big impact on the people for the king to notice it and then share it in this psalm.

If God has ever led you away from trouble and offered the calm assurance that He loves you enough to step into messy places and rescue you, tell Him you noticed.

LET ME LIVE WITH THE FEELING OF CALM THAT YOU GAVE YOUR PEOPLE LONG AGO, LORD. HELP ME REMEMBER TO ASK YOU FOR HELP WHEN THE STRUGGLE BUS SHOWS UP OFFERING FREE TRANSPORTATION TO THE FEELING OF RAGE.

JOY AND PEACE

Being with You is to be full of joy. In Your right hand there is happiness forever.
PSALM 16:11 NLV

If you want to be calm, you need to get close to God. He's the only one who can change difficult days into peaceful, joyful experiences.

Of course, you're welcome to try to do it on your own, but you'll never be as successful as God. You can try to change your behavior, but God really wants to change your heart. A feeling of calm arrives when you follow Him. As you journey with God day by day, He fills you with joy, peace, and contentment.

Keep in mind that a lot of things can make you happy, so happiness isn't always the best goal to have. It's not that God doesn't want you to be happy, but He does want you to make sure that the things you choose to make you happy are things that He has provided—His blessings and not just things that amuse or entertain you.

KEEP ME CLOSE, FATHER. REMIND ME TO COME BACK TO YOU IF I START GETTING OFF TRACK. BRING A FEELING OF CALM ON THE HARD DAYS I FACE.

BOREDOM AND RESPONSIBILITY

Lazy people sleep soundly,
but idleness leaves them hungry.
PROVERBS 19:15 NLT

Everyone wants to sleep well at night. But sometimes feeling guilty, angry, or discouraged means that your mind spends time thinking about what caused these feelings—and then it can be hard to sleep. If you're feeling bored, then you might sleep very well. You can't find anything else to do, so sleep comes easily.

But who wants to feel bored? When you feel this way, the remedy is to do something worthwhile. Don't use your time to get into trouble. You might think that you deserve free time without any need to be responsible, but that's not part of growing up. As you get older, you'll have more responsibilities and more jobs to finish. You might begin to make choices that break God's rules if you let the feeling of boredom steer your thoughts and ideas. Whenever the feeling of boredom sets in, ask God to help you.

WHEN I DON'T WANT TO DO ANYTHING—FOR MYSELF OR TO HELP OTHERS—HELP ME, FATHER. I DON'T WANT THIS FEELING TO KEEP ME FROM GROWING UP AND BEING RESPONSIBLE.

Boredom Fighters

Whatever your hand finds to do,
do it with all your strength.
ECCLESIASTES 9:10 NLV

When you want to get rid of the feeling of boredom, find someone who needs your help—ask a family member, a neighbor, or a friend. God says that hard work is a good thing. When you help others, you're showing initiative. *Initiative* is a big word that means you noticed something that needed to be done, and you decided to do it. It might not be a job you were asked to do, but initiative shows love, kindness, and care that go much further than words.

You should never do just a "passable" job. The work you do should always be your best work. Pay attention to details, aim to finish what you start, and give more than you might want to. The work you do is to be done like you're doing it for God—so do it well.

TEACH ME INITIATIVE WHEN I FEEL BORED, GOD.
HELP ME NOTICE WHEN OTHER PEOPLE NEED HELP AND
THEN HELP WHEN I CAN. WHEN I DO A TASK, HELP ME DO
IT AS IF YOU ASKED SO I'LL REMEMBER TO DO MY BEST.

IF YOU TRULY WANT TO KNOW GOD, YOU'LL NEED TO TURN DOWN THE VOLUME ON EVERYTHING THAT ISN'T HIM—AND LISTEN FOR HIS VOICE.

TURN DOWN THE VOLUME

He says, "Be still, and know that I am God."
PSALM 46:10 NIV

There's a very simple yet very hard way to feel calm. What you need to do is be still and think about God. See? *Simple.* The hard part is that so many things compete for your attention. Other feelings seem to take over and shove the feeling of calm to the bottom of the stack.

When you take time to be with God, it can seem like just one of many things you have to do. Sometimes you might even forget to make time for Him. Other feelings might encourage you to stray away from your journey with Him. You might think there are just too many things to do.

Time seems pretty important (and it is!). You want to fill it with fun and productive things. But if you truly want to know God, you'll need to turn down the volume on everything that isn't Him—and listen for His voice.

SOMETIMES I FEEL LIKE I'M MISSING OUT ON THINGS IF I SPEND TOO MUCH TIME WITH YOU, LORD. REMIND ME THAT WHEN I WANT TO FEEL CALM, I NEED TO GET CLOSE TO YOU.

SHOW INITIATIVE—SHOW LOVE

Indolence wants it all and gets nothing;
the energetic have something to show for their lives.
PROVERBS 13:4 MSG

Did you stumble over that first word in today's verse? *Indolence* means to be bored and unwilling to help. If you're indolent, it means you want something but aren't willing to work for it.

Feeling bored might mean you say, "Why try?" or "Who cares?" or "I just don't want to help." A bored person lets others do the work because they don't want to. When you think this way, other people won't feel kindness toward you when you could help but choose not to.

There may be a good reason you're unable to help (you had something else you promised to help with, or the work is something you can't physically do). But when you *can* help but choose *not* to, you fail to show initiative (noticing something that could be done and doing it to the best of your ability), and you fail to show the same love that God shows you.

HELP ME LOOK MORE LIKE YOU, LORD. YOU'VE HELPED ME—PLEASE GUIDE ME IN HELPING OTHERS.

NO DOWNTIME?

Flee the evil desires of youth and pursue righteousness, faith, love and peace, along with those who call on the Lord out of a pure heart.
2 TIMOTHY 2:22 NIV

When you feel bored, today's verse gives you four great choices for figuring out how to handle it. When you have something to do, get up and chase the things that God said would lead to right living. These include *faith* to believe God's Word is true, *love* for those you meet, and *peace* in knowing there was something to do and you did it.

It might seem like you don't have any time to rest, but that's not true. God wants you to be still enough to learn from Him, but if you're honest, you'll admit there are times when you do nothing and have no interest in learning from God.

Quiet your heart and spend time with God, then ask Him what special thing He'd like you to do when you feel bored.

POINT MY FEET IN THE DIRECTION OF GOOD CHOICES AND RIGHT LIVING, FATHER. WHEN I HAVE DOWNTIME, HELP ME LEARN THE THINGS YOU WANT TO TEACH ME.

PRAISE AND WORSHIP

Those who live at the ends of the earth stand in awe of your wonders. From where the sun rises to where it sets, you inspire shouts of joy.
PSALM 65:8 NLT

Did you know that praise is a choice? Did you know that worship is also a choice? By choosing to praise and worship, you might discover some new feelings. But praise and worship aren't things you feel; they're choices you make to honor God.

What is it about spending time praising God and worshipping Him that can make you feel something called *awe*? This three-letter word means to be filled with feelings of respect and wonder. It means you recognize that God is good, that what He does is amazing, and that how He works is unexpected. Because God does more for you than anyone else ever could or would, you're encouraged to feel awe when you think of Him.

WHEN I WORSHIP AND WHEN I PRAISE YOU, GOD, GIVE ME A SENSE OF AWE AT WHO YOU ARE AND HOW YOU CONTINUE TO WORK IN MY LIFE.

More Impressive

Let all the people of the world honor [God].
Psalm 33:8 NLV

Not every person will feel awe toward God. Some might feel awe about a beautiful mountain, a pine-green forest, or a swirling ocean. After all, these are all bigger and more inspiring than most of the things people experience every day.

But God said there will be a time when every person on the planet will feel a sense of awe for God. Awe is a feeling that God wants everyone to have, so He made sure everyone will feel it. They might experience it now—or later. But *everyone* will have this feeling about God.

God is so much more impressive than anything you could imagine. He's more amazing than video games, musicians, or sports. You'll always stay closer to God when you feel the awe that leads you to follow, honor, and obey Him.

I DON'T WANT TO WAIT TO HONOR YOU AND FEEL AWE, LORD. I WANT TO SEE THE BEAUTY OF EVERYTHING YOU'VE MADE AND THEN THINK ABOUT HOW AMAZING AND WONDERFUL YOU ARE!

WRITTEN FOR YOU

My awe at your words keeps me stable.
PSALM 119:161 MSG

The feeling of awe comes when you choose to think about how amazing God is and how impressive His creation is. . .and awe can even be discovered in the words you read in the Bible.

Some people don't read the Bible because they think it's too hard, too big, or too old. But the author of Psalm 119 said his awe at God's words kept him stable. That means by paying attention to God's words, he felt calm and at peace.

You might have memories of encouraging things people have said to you; their words meant a lot. These good memories can help you feel calm and peaceful for a while. But the Bible is God's Word written for every human who has ever lived, and it is personal, helpful, and filled with good news. You can feel awe at knowing that the words you read were written *for* you *by* God.

YOUR WORDS ARE IMPORTANT, FATHER. I WANT TO READ THEM AND EXPERIENCE THE AWE OF KNOWING THAT YOU WROTE THESE WORDS FOR ME.

MIGHTY AND AWESOME

The LORD your God is God of gods and Lord of lords, the great God, mighty and awesome.
DEUTERONOMY 10:17 NIV

Think of all the people you know. Are any of them greater than God? Think about all the leaders you've ever learned about in school. Were any of them wiser than God? Think about the strongest person you've ever heard of. Are they stronger than God? No one is greater, wiser, or stronger. *No one*. God is the mightiest and most awesome.

When you feel awe, it's because you've compared God to everything and everyone else and know that nothing and no one will ever come close to deserving the honor and wonder that belong to Him.

The feeling of awe begins with learning what God has said and continues as you think about what He has done. Reflecting on His awesomeness will lead you to speak words of praise, thanksgiving, and worship to God and inspire a feeling of awe for the one who has always loved you.

THE FEELING OF AWE IS ONE OF THE BEST FEELINGS I CAN HAVE, GOD. YOUR LOVE FOR ME IS AMAZING. THANK YOU.

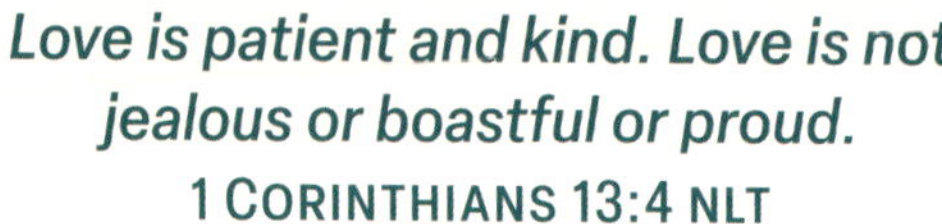

THE TWO SIDES OF A COIN

Love is patient and kind. Love is not jealous or boastful or proud.
1 CORINTHIANS 13:4 NLT

There are two sides to a coin. Most of the time, one side looks very different from the other. One side is considered the front (heads), while the other is known as the back (tails). You don't have to look very long before you can spot the difference between the sides.

Jealousy (also known as envy) is part of a two-sided coin. Compassion (also known as love) is on the flip side. Everything related to jealousy is very different from everything related to love. Love is patient and kind, but feelings of jealousy can cause you to pretend to be proud. You might want to tell others how important you are, even when you think they might be more important. When you're jealous, you don't like it when someone else is successful and you're not. You don't want anyone other than you to be recognized.

Love starts as a choice and can become a feeling. Likewise, jealousy is both a choice and a feeling. Choose love.

I DON'T EVER WANT TO CHOOSE JEALOUSY, LORD. INSTEAD, HELP ME TO CHOOSE LOVE EACH DAY. MAKE ME PATIENT AND KIND LIKE YOU ARE.

1 CORINTHIANS 13:4

Love is patient and kind. Love is not jealous or boastful or proud.

YOU'RE AN ORIGINAL

We will not compare ourselves with each other as if one of us were better and another worse. We have far more interesting things to do with our lives. Each of us is an original.

GALATIANS 5:26 MSG

Do you find yourself comparing the good things you do with bad things other people do? This can lead to the feeling of pride. Do you compare the bad things you do with good things other people do? This can lead to the feeling of jealousy. Comparison is a choice that can lead to some very unhelpful feelings.

Instead of comparing yourself to others, you can compare what you do with what God does and stir up feelings of gratitude. Because you're an original, there's never a need to compare yourself to any other human. God doesn't look at people that way. He doesn't love one person more and another less because of their talents or their abilities or even the choices they make.

Stop comparing. You have way better things to do with your life.

THANK YOU FOR LOVING ME, GOD. AND THANK YOU FOR SHOWING ME THAT I NEVER NEED TO FEEL JEALOUS BECAUSE YOU ACCEPT ME JUST AS I AM.

GOD'S INSTRUCTIONS

Rid yourselves of all malice and all deceit, hypocrisy, envy, and slander of every kind.
1 PETER 2:1 NIV

When feelings of jealousy arrive, tell them to keep moving. *You don't need them*. You shouldn't want them. They'll never help you. Jealousy (envy) hangs out with malice (hate), deceit (lies), hypocrisy (dishonesty), and slander (making up untrue stories about people and sharing them with others as if they are true).

None of these choices bring feelings that will help you love others, God, or the truth. Each of them, however, can cause you to make up stories in which you're the hero and everyone else is an enemy.

If you send these choices away, there will be a lot of bad feelings that have no reason to stick around.

God *always* gives instructions for a reason. It's never to keep you from doing what you want to do. Instead, His instructions can help you learn to make better choices that lead to a better life.

BAD FEELINGS MAKE HORRIBLE COMPANY, LORD. KEEP THEM FAR FROM ME. HELP ME TRUST YOUR INSTRUCTIONS SO I ALWAYS SEEK TO MAKE GOOD CHOICES THAT LEAD TO GOOD FEELINGS.

CHANGiNG HeARTS

Always be humble and gentle. Be patient with each other, making allowance for each .other's faults because of your love.

EPHESIANS 4:2 NLT

Everyone wants to feel accepted. You do too. And so you do your best to fit in. You try to guess what others want you to do and then do it. The problem is that by trying to fit in (be accepted), you might make some choices that God warned against.

God wants you to accept people and let Him do any changing that He thinks is best. Be patient with other people and be patient with yourself. Love other people and allow God to love you. You know that there are good choices to make, so you can let God help you make them. He will do the same for others.

Loving other people will do more to help them change than telling them all the things they've done wrong. God can change a heart—and you can show others His love.

HELP ME REMEMBER THAT IF I WANT TO BE ACCEPTED, OTHER PEOPLE DO TOO, FATHER. EVERYONE BREAKS YOUR RULES, BUT EVERYONE CAN ALSO BE ACCEPTED BY YOU. CHANGE MY HEART. CHANGE THEIRS TOO.

Jesus Loves Everyone

Peter said to them. . ."God has shown me I should not say that any man is unclean."
ACTS 10:28 NLV

Peter was a disciple (follower) of Jesus. He'd heard Jesus speak and was there when Jesus was led away to die on a cross. But Peter found it very hard to believe that Jesus loved everyone. He thought God only loved the people who were from his nation. Peter thought other people should be left out; he thought they should never feel accepted by God. God had to do some extra work to help Peter understand that He wanted *every* man, woman, boy, and girl to know that they could feel accepted by Him and should be accepted by people who follow Him.

God doesn't want anyone to feel left out. He sent Jesus to rescue people—that includes each person who accepts Him. God didn't leave anyone out. He doesn't want you to leave anyone out either.

EVERYONE NEEDS TO FEEL ACCEPTED BY YOU, GOD. NO ONE IS PERFECT WHEN YOU SEEK THEM—BUT YOU CAN CHANGE PEOPLE BECAUSE YOU LOVE THEM FIRST.

WHAT MAKES YOU DIFFERENT?

Be ready to speak up and tell anyone who asks why you're living the way you are, and always with the utmost courtesy.
1 PETER 3:15 MSG

People might want to know what makes you different. They might be wondering if you would even accept them because you make different (or better) choices than they do. Either you can show them love or you can make it clear that you think they're unacceptable.

When you share what you're learning about God, be careful not to make others feel guilty. You never need to change the story of God's good news, but you may need to understand that other people might not know everything that you know about God. God wants you to tell them. . .but do it with love and acceptance.

The feeling of acceptance is one of the best ways for people to come to know God. Don't try to make people feel as if God has no interest in loving them. When Jesus came, He proved that God loves *everyone*.

I WANT TO SHARE YOUR LOVE, LORD. TEACH ME TO BE KIND AND NOT DEMANDING, LOVING AND NOT JUDGING, CARING AND NOT CRITICIZING.

The Golden Rule

"In everything, do to others what you would have them do to you, for this sums up the Law and the Prophets."
MATTHEW 7:12 NIV

Did you know that you just read the "Golden Rule"? Making others feel accepted is a big part of this rule. You're asked to treat others the same way you would like to be treated. If you don't want people to be rude to you, then you shouldn't be rude to other people. If you want people to be kind, then be kind first.

God's rules are all about caring enough for others that they feel accepted in the same way you want to be accepted. Even if they are rude in return? *Yes.* Even if they are unkind? *Yes.* Even when they never treat you the way you treat them? *Yes.*

There's something beautiful about loving others the way God loves you. It shows acceptance—God always accepts you, doesn't He? You can help others feel accepted by God too.

I WANT TO TELL PEOPLE MORE ABOUT HOW YOU MAKE THINGS RIGHT, FATHER. I WANT THE PEOPLE I MEET TO FEEL ACCEPTED BY YOU.

New Feelings Welcome

I praise God for what he has promised.
I trust in God, so why should I be afraid?
What can mere mortals do to me?
PSALM 56:4 NLT

You've been learning that feelings affect the choices you make. But the choices you make will also bring feelings. In Psalm 56, King David wrote that he made a choice to trust the promise God made. The choice to believe God can send feelings of fear and depression packing. And it brings new feelings to the surface, like confidence and awe.

What if David hadn't made the choice to believe? It's likely that his feelings of fear and depression were what the king could expect. God is aware that people will feel depressed sometimes, but He made sure there are choices you can make to help your feeling of depression lessen over time.

You never need to act on your negative feelings, but those feelings can remind you to make a new choice so you can welcome new, better feelings.

TEACH ME HOW TO AVOID CERTAIN FEELINGS THROUGH THE CHOICES I MAKE, GOD. HELP ME REMEMBER THAT FEELINGS ARE NOT THE BOSS OF MY CHOICES.

SPARE ROOM

"Call on Me in the day of trouble. I will take you out of trouble, and you will honor Me."
PSALM 50:15 NLV

When you feel unhappy, you can look to God's Word for instructions that will help you change things. For one, *pray*. God says He can take you out of the trouble you face. When He does, expect to feel a sense of awe.

Seems pretty easy, doesn't it? But maybe it's something you've never done before. When most people are unhappy, they don't make new choices that can change their feelings. They just keep hanging out with unhappiness and wonder if it will ever go away.

The truth is, you'll continue to experience feelings you don't like for the rest of your life, but you never need to give them the spare room in your heart.

If you find it hard to spend time with unhappy people, then you should do something to make sure *you* aren't the unhappy person whom others try to avoid. Talk to God and honor Him when He removes your unhappiness.

IT'S HARD TO THINK I CAN BE ANYTHING BUT UNHAPPY WHEN BAD THINGS HAPPEN, LORD. BUT YOU'RE HERE. I WANT TO ACCEPT YOUR HELP.

Feelings are a bit like the various colors a painter uses to create a beautiful picture. Not all the colors are used equally, but all of them will be used at some point.

FEELING COLORS

Weeping may stay for the night,
but rejoicing comes in the morning.
PSALM 30:5 NIV

Did you know that every bad feeling has an expiration date? If you're weighed down by discouragement, it won't last. That's true for anger, fear, and tension too. Today, if you're swamped by sorrow, be encouraged by knowing it won't last forever. You don't have to make a choice based on a temporary feeling.

A lot of people are sad, and sometimes the feeling is so strong that they make choices that could harm themselves or others because they mistakenly think the feeling will never leave—but it will.

Feelings are a bit like the various colors a painter uses to create a beautiful picture. Not all the colors are used equally, but all of them will be used at some point.

God gave you feelings, and each one can remind you that God cares about how you feel and gives you good advice in His Word—and He *always* tells you the truth.

ANYTIME I FEEL SOMETHING BAD, I NEED TO REMEMBER I WON'T FEEL THAT WAY FOREVER. GOD, GIVE ME THE COURAGE TO BELIEVE MY UNHAPPINESS WILL END.

GOD'S PROTECTION

The LORD is a shelter for the oppressed,
a refuge in times of trouble.
PSALM 9:9 NLT

This verse from the Psalms offers a wonderful reminder that you have a place to go when you're unhappy. It won't be a place where you feel even more depressed. You see, bad feelings often encourage other bad feelings. If you don't do something to stop the cycle, you'll continue to feel worse. But there's a better way.

Psalm 9 says that God can offer protection when the bad choices of others cheer you on in making the same type of bad choices. You don't need to follow their advice. Unhappiness isn't a great place to live.

God can provide safety, give you comfort, and offer instructions for staying away from (or leaving) unhappiness. If you want to get away from unhappiness, check in with the God who can change your "feelings" destination.

I DON'T KNOW WHY I SOMETIMES SETTLE FOR BEING UNHAPPY, LORD. CHANGE MY THINKING SO I CAN MAKE THE CHOICE TO LEAVE WHERE I AM FOR WHERE YOU ARE.

TAKE A DEEP DIVE

Worry in the heart of a man weighs it down, but a good word makes it glad.

PROVERBS 12:25 NLV

There are different shades, or levels, of happiness. You might feel joy, excitement, or cheer. When you're happy, you believe good things will happen, and you'd like to stay happy forever. (Avoid jumping into the deep waters of a feeling that is far from happiness—and steer clear of worrying about things you can't control.)

There's a way you can help others feel happiness too. Sure, you could tell them a joke that makes them laugh, but the best way is to encourage them. Good feelings can be encouraged just like your good choices can lead to better feelings. So make the good choice of encouragement. It often leads to happiness or joy—for you and for others!

IT'S TRUE, I WANT TO BE HAPPY, FATHER. HELP ME SAY NO TO WORRY, AND HELP ME ENCOURAGE OTHERS SO MORE PEOPLE CAN KNOW YOU.

CHOOSE CHEERFUL

A cheerful disposition is good for your health;
gloom and doom leave you bone-tired.
PROVERBS 17:22 MSG

Do you greet people with a smile? Maybe you're a bit sarcastic or rude. Your attitude can change the way others feel. Your words and actions can actually steal happiness from others. But your negative feelings also do something to you. The Bible says a gloom-and-doom outlook will leave you bone-tired.

When you don't notice the good in anything because you're too busy being negative, then you miss out on the wonder of all that God has made. You might even begin to make fun of good things. It's so much better to be cheerful. Bringing a cheerful attitude to your interactions with others may be unexpected, but it will definitely be appreciated. Such an outlook welcomes smiles and positive feelings.

Be cheerful. . .because people need it.

I MAY NOT BE ABLE TO CHOOSE HOW I FEEL, GOD, BUT I CAN CHOOSE HOW I RESPOND. HELP ME BE CHEERFUL AND LET YOU DELIVER THE RIGHT FEELINGS.

Filling the Feeling Tank

You make known to me the path of life;
you will fill me with joy in your presence,
with eternal pleasures at your right hand.
PSALM 16:11 NIV

You might think of joy as something different than happiness. They seem like they should be the same thing, but joy is a feeling that God is good no matter how hard things are. Happiness, on the other hand, is all about responding to the good things that happen to you. On a good day, you might be happy; on a hard day, though, you can still feel joy even when nothing seems to go your way.

Psalm 16:11 talks about joy. God fills your feeling tank by staying close even when you have a broken heart or someone has betrayed you. Good things come to boys who stay close to God. Happiness is the way you respond to good news; joy is the right response to God's goodness.

HELP ME FEEL SATISFIED WHEN I'M HAPPY, LORD. MAY I BE EVEN MORE SATISFIED WHEN I'M CLOSE ENOUGH TO YOU TO FEEL JOY.

THE HONOR OF FEELING JOY

Because of our faith, Christ has brought us into this place of undeserved privilege where we now stand, and we confidently and joyfully look forward to sharing God's glory.

ROMANS 5:2 NLT

Let's take a deeper look at Romans 5:2.

Because of our faith—this is a choice *and* a hint of something good that happens while you follow Jesus.

Christ has brought us into this place of undeserved privilege—you're given permission to come close to God.

We confidently and joyfully look forward to sharing God's glory—the good things God has planned may not happen today, but they *will* happen, and you can be confident knowing that God's promise will come true. This choice is what will bring joy on your uncertain days.

Some days you can be happy and cheerful. . .and other days you have the honor of feeling joy because you know God is good and things will get better.

HELP ME TO APPRECIATE BEING CHEERFUL AND HAPPY, FATHER. AND THANK YOU FOR THE HONOR OF EXPERIENCING YOUR JOY AS I CHOOSE TO BELIEVE WHAT YOU'VE SAID AND LOOK FORWARD TO THE GOOD THINGS YOU HAVE IN STORE FOR ME.

CONNECTED TO YOUR CHOICES

Is anyone among you suffering?
He should pray. Is anyone happy?
He should sing songs of thanks to God.
JAMES 5:13 NLV

Now that you've learned about the difference between the feelings of joy and happiness, you can probably pick out what feeling God had in mind when you read these words in scripture: "Is anyone among you suffering?" That person is invited to pray to a good God—and to experience *joy* as a result. On the other hand, when we're happy, we can respond by singing songs of praise and gratitude.

With joy you can feel satisfaction and peace. With happiness you can feel delight and optimism. Joy can always be part of your response, while happiness is a short-term feeling.

The choices you make can lead to good feelings or bad feelings. You're quickly learning how some of those feelings are connected to your choices.

THANK YOU FOR ALL THE FEELINGS, GOD. EACH FEELING GIVES ME THE CHANCE TO ASK FOR HELP—OR TO SAY THANKS. EITHER WAY, I'M REMINDED OF YOU.

HARD TIMES, EXHAUSTING DAYS

Don't you know anything? Haven't you been listening? God doesn't come and go. God lasts. He's Creator of all you can see or imagine. He doesn't get tired out, doesn't pause to catch his breath. And he knows everything, inside and out. He energizes those who get tired.

ISAIAH 40:28–29 MSG

God isn't an energy drink, but He can make you feel energized. Feeling exhausted is normal. After all, you might play sports or work hard outside, or maybe you had a long day of schoolwork. God doesn't get tired but knows that you do. He doesn't sleep but knows that you must. He doesn't become discouraged but knows that you will.

Take the time to step away from feelings of weariness, exhaustion, and stress. These feelings often leave you thinking about choices God never wants you to make. There's never a need to give up or walk out.

God doesn't expect you to go without sleep, but He teaches ways you can endure hard times on tiring days.

WHEN DIFFICULTIES SEEM TOO HARD AND I'M WORN OUT, HELP ME, LORD. THANK YOU FOR REMINDING ME THAT YOU CAN DO WHAT I CAN'T. THANKS FOR ALWAYS HELPING ME.

BUSY EPAPHRODITUS

I think it is necessary to send back to you Epaphroditus, my brother, co-worker and fellow soldier, who is also your messenger, whom you sent to take care of my needs. For he longs for all of you and is distressed because you heard he was ill.

PHILIPPIANS 2:25–26 NIV

You may have never heard of Epaphroditus, but he must have been a very busy man. The apostle Paul had very kind things to say about him. Paul called him a brother, a coworker, a fellow soldier in God's army, and a messenger. Epaphroditus had spent time and energy helping Paul. He wanted to head back home, but he was ill. Many believe Epaphroditus was exhausted. He had many jobs, and he did them all to the best of his ability—until he was so worn out he became sick.

This kind of exhausted feeling might also be called stress. It can seem like there's never enough time to do all the things you need to do. Sometimes the feeling of exhaustion might cause you to make the choice to stop, listen, and be refreshed. And that's *always* the right choice.

WHEN I FEEL EXHAUSTED, HELP ME BE STILL
SO I CAN PAY ATTENTION TO YOU, FATHER.

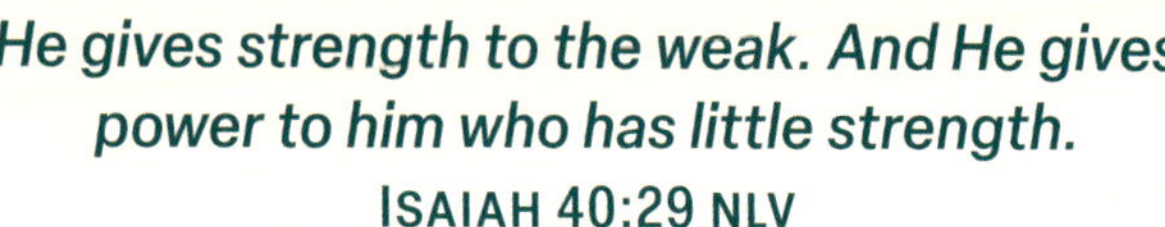

The Help You Need Most

He gives strength to the weak. And He gives power to him who has little strength.
ISAIAH 40:29 NLV

If you ever think no one cares how you feel, you would be wrong. God cares! He cares about the way you feel and pays close attention to every choice you make.

You'll face a lot of challenges in life. Some will be harder than others and you'll get exhausted dealing with them. But God uses downtime to help you discover ways to be refreshed before your next great adventure or challenge. It's good to have a mix of busyness and downtime, because if you're always resting, you'll lose sight of what God wants you to do. And if you're always busy, you won't have time to notice the things God wants you to pay attention to.

When you feel exhausted, admit it—to yourself and to God. He already knows how you feel, but He wants you to understand that He'll step in and help when you need it—so be sure to ask Him for His help!

SOMETIMES I'M TIRED AND I DON'T REALLY KNOW WHY, LORD. BE WITH ME, TEACH ME, AND WALK WITH ME INTO OUR NEXT ADVENTURE. BUT FIRST, GIVE ME REST.

He gives strength to the weak. And He gives power to him who has little strength.

THE GAME OF A LIFETIME

Recognize what [God] wants from you, and quickly respond to it. Unlike the culture around you, always dragging you down to its level of immaturity, God brings the best out of you, develops well-formed maturity in you.

ROMANS 12:2 MSG

If a coach puts you into a football game, does he expect you to remain on the sidelines watching the other players? If you're in choir, does the director expect you to just stand there? Everything you're a part of requires action.

There's no reason for you to stay on the sidelines if you're part of a sports team. You're expected to use your voice when you sing in a choir. In the same way, if you're a Christian, you're expected to play an active role in following God instead of experiencing the adventure from someone else's perspective.

Be energized because God is helping you grow into an amazing young man. When God has something for you to do, *respond*. You're in the game of a lifetime, and God has a plan for victory.

I WANT TO BE READY WHEN YOU CALL MY NAME, FATHER. I CAN'T WAIT TO SEE WHAT YOU HAVE PLANNED FOR ME.

PERSONAL TRAINER

I pray that out of his glorious riches he may strengthen you with power through his Spirit in your inner being.
EPHESIANS 3:16 NIV

God didn't create you to do life alone. Everyone needs help at times, and no one is so strong that they don't need God's help. Drinking soda with caffeine won't give you the strength you need. Working out at the gym won't be enough. You need a personal trainer—but not just any personal trainer. The one who can train you is also the God who can give you the strength you need to feel energized and ready for adventure.

The strength you need doesn't come from lifting weights at the gym—this strength runs deep, and it helps you face difficult moments. It allows you to help others who struggle too.

God has everything you need.

WHEN I'M DOING WHAT YOU MADE ME TO DO, I FEEL ENERGIZED, GOD. BE MY PERSONAL TRAINER AND RESOURCE MANAGER SO I CAN DO WHAT YOU CREATED ME TO DO.

LOOKING BEYOND TROUBLE

We don't look at the troubles we can see now; rather, we fix our gaze on things that cannot be seen. For the things we see now will soon be gone, but the things we cannot see will last forever.

2 CORINTHIANS 4:18 NLT

The things you experience in life aren't always great. It can seem like one bad thing brings more bad things. You see it. . .you feel it. . .but you don't like it. You don't want struggle to be a part of your story. Yet it's there whether you want it or not.

God wants you to feel energized by looking *beyond* trouble. Life on earth will always include hard things, but God said His future plans for you are perfect and will last forever. Looking beyond what you're feeling today will help you feel differently about the trouble you're experiencing right now. Why? Trouble won't last forever, but God's goodness will.

WHEN BAD THINGS HAPPEN, THEY OFTEN GET ALL MY ATTENTION, LORD. HELP ME UNDERSTAND THAT BETTER THINGS ARE AHEAD. AND HELP ME BE PATIENT WHILE I WAIT FOR THEM.

THE VERY BEST WORK

Whatever work you do, do it with all your heart. Do it for the Lord and not for men.
COLOSSIANS 3:23 NLV

If you want to feel energized, remember that God gave you a reason to feel this way. When you have a big job to do and you want to do what is worthwhile, it helps to remember why you're doing something that might seem hard.

Maybe your mom or dad asked you to do something, and when you actually do the work you feel energized by reminding yourself of this: The work you do is so much better when you're doing it for God. With this truth in mind, you'll have a better attitude while doing the work. You'll work harder and be happier while doing it.

Like so many feelings, being energized begins with a choice. . .even though you may have been dragging your feet when you started.

IF I'M ASKED TO DO SOMETHING, HELP ME FEEL HONORED AND ENERGIZED, FATHER. I WANT TO DO MY VERY BEST WORK—FOR YOU.

PAUL'S WEAKNESS

Each time he said, "My grace is all you need. My power works best in weakness." So now I am glad to boast about my weaknesses, so that the power of Christ can work through me.

2 CORINTHIANS 12:9 NLT

The apostle Paul is remembered for being bold—he didn't seem to fear others. But Paul also had something he called a "thorn in the flesh." He never said what this "thorn" was, but most people believe it was a struggle that he couldn't do anything about. This struggle made Paul feel weak.

Paul asked God to take the struggle away, but God said no. Instead, He gave Paul a new gift when he felt weak: Paul received grace through a close friendship with God.

Paul knew that when he was strong, it was only because God made him that way.

HELP ME NEVER BE AFRAID TO ADMIT THAT I'M WEAK, GOD. PLEASE USE YOUR STRENGTH TO HELP ME DO THINGS I CAN'T DO ON MY OWN.

GOD UNDERSTANDS YOUR WEAKNESS

The Holy Spirit helps us where we are weak. We do not know how to pray or what we should pray for, but the Holy Spirit prays to God for us.

ROMANS 8:26 NLV

Maybe you've seen people helping people. One is weak and the other is strong. When the weak person accepts the help of the strong person, they get where they need to go much faster. When the strong help those who feel weak, this act of kindness always begins with the choice to love. Seeing this kind of help is encouraging.

God does the same for you when you feel weak. You may be struggling so much that you can't even begin to pray. God even planned for this struggle by having His Spirit pray for you when you can't find the words. God understands your weakness. And because He loves you, He kindly offers His strength even when you aren't strong enough to ask for His help.

WHEN THE WORDS DON'T COME, WILL YOUR SPIRIT PRAY FOR ME, LORD? WHEN I'M WEAK, HELP ME BELIEVE IN YOUR STRENGTH.

A FRIENDSHIP WITH WEAKNESS

That is why, for Christ's sake, I delight in weaknesses, in insults, in hardships, in persecutions, in difficulties. For when I am weak, then I am strong.
2 CORINTHIANS 12:10 NIV

It's sad, but sometimes people will pick on those who are weaker. They like being seen as strong, but they act like bullies. Aren't you glad that's not what God does? He sees every time someone hurts you, and He knows when life is difficult for you. God is aware of the challenges you face each day.

The apostle Paul wrote something very curious. He said that he "delighted" in weakness. In his weakness, he trusted that God would step in and take over with His strength. This feeling was a great reminder that Paul didn't face trouble alone.

HELP ME TO KNOW YOU'RE WITH ME WHEN I'M WEAK, FATHER. I LOOK FORWARD TO WATCHING YOU DO GREAT THINGS IN MY LIFE BECAUSE YOU'RE SO STRONG.

WHAT YOU SHOULD DO NEXT

Let us come boldly to the throne of our gracious God. There we will receive his mercy, and we will find grace to help us when we need it most.

HEBREWS 4:16 NLT

You might feel tired, weary, exhausted. . . There's another feeling to add to this list—*weak*. You want to do your best work for God. You want to be a good example to others around you. You want to do more—but sometimes you need to admit that you're weak. You don't always have what it takes to do what needs to be done, not on your own anyway. You need help.

Weakness is usually combined with at least one other feeling. For example, you can feel weak and sad. You can feel weak and angry. You can feel weak and desperate. Why? Most people don't like to feel weak, so that feeling brings along other bad feelings. But God wants something better for you. He said that the feeling of weakness should partner with the feeling of confidence in Him. Come to God when you need help, and He'll always come to your rescue.

WHEN I'M WEAK, HELP ME FEEL CONFIDENT ENOUGH TO ASK FOR YOUR HELP, GOD. THERE ARE SOME THINGS I JUST CAN'T DO ON MY OWN.

When you look to God for help to do the unexpected, His strength will become *your* strength.

DO THE WORK

"'Now be strong, Zerubbabel,' says the Lord. 'Be strong, Joshua son of Jehozadak, head religious leader. And be strong, all you people of the land,' says the Lord. 'Do the work, for I am with you,' says the Lord of All."

HAGGAI 2:4 NLV

It was a bad time for the people of Israel. Horrible decisions had been made, so God stepped in to issue a national time-out. The temple couldn't be used. It needed to be rebuilt. But there were few people to do the work. It was discouraging.

God wanted His people to feel strong. Three times in Haggai 2:4, God tells someone (or a group) to "be strong." God was encouraging them, but the people had a choice. . .and their decision to be strong would soon become a feeling.

God might not ask you to do something you already know how to do. Sometimes He asks you to do something and you have no idea how you'll get it done. You feel clueless. But when you say yes to Him—when you look to Him for help to do the unexpected—His strength will become *your* strength.

I FEEL STRONG WHEN I OBEY YOU, LORD. HELP ME TO DO WHAT YOU ASK—EVEN IF I'VE NEVER DONE IT BEFORE.

GOD WANTS YOU TO BE STRONG

For we do not have a high priest who is unable to empathize with our weaknesses, but we have one who has been tempted in every way, just as we are—yet he did not sin.
HEBREWS 4:15 NIV

God knows what it's like to feel strong—He is strong all the time. But God also understands weakness. You see, He sent Jesus to earth, and Jesus faced the same kinds of struggles that you do today. While Jesus always made the right choice, He still experienced what it felt like to be weak. There were times when Jesus was physically weak, and there were times when He was emotionally weak.

It shouldn't be a surprise that the God who knows what weakness is like wants you to be strong. He knows that people who feel weak can also feel defeated, sad, and lonely. He doesn't want that for you, because He knows if you accept Him into your heart, you are never defeated or left alone. With Him by your side, you are victorious!

I'M GRATEFUL THAT WHEN I'M WEAK YOU UNDERSTAND WHAT I'M FEELING, GOD. YOU WANT TO MAKE ME STRONG. HELP ME ACCEPT THE STRENGTH YOU OFFER.

REMEMBERING GOD'S GOODNESS

The Lord stood with me and gave me strength.
2 TIMOTHY 4:17 NLT

The apostle Paul wrote two letters to a young man named Timothy to help him learn more about God. Paul had a very good opinion of Timothy and wrote to him about a struggle he had faced. Another man named Alexander had hurt him. Men who Paul had thought were his friends had left him, and Paul thought he was going to die. But through it all, God stood with Paul and gave him strength.

It was important for Paul to remember God's goodness. And it was important for him to remind Timothy that God could transform times of weakness into testimonies of God's strength.

Just like Paul, you can share your weak-to-strong stories with others. Your testimony might be just what other people need to hear because they're tired of feeling weak too.

YOU RESCUE PEOPLE, LORD. THEY NEED TO HEAR ME SHARE ABOUT THE TIMES YOU'VE RESCUED ME. THEY ALSO NEED TO HEAR ME SAY THAT WHEN THEY'RE WEAK, YOU CAN HELP THEM FEEL STRONG.

TAKE A HARD PASS

Keep away from everything that even looks like sin.
1 THESSALONIANS 5:22 NLV

There are certain things God wants you to feel serious about. It's safe to say that He wants you to feel serious about Him, His Word (the Bible), and His rules. If you feel serious about God, then you won't ignore Him or act like what He says isn't very important.

The apostle Paul told the people of the church in Thessalonica that if they felt serious about God, they would stay away from everything that even *looked* like sin. If it seemed like it might break God's rules, the people should say no and take a hard pass on it.

If you want to be serious about following God, then take time to read more about Him. Do what He asks and be grateful for His instructions.

FOLLOWING YOU IS SERIOUS BUSINESS, FATHER. HELP ME HONOR YOU BY TAKING YOU AND YOUR INSTRUCTIONS SERIOUSLY, AND GIVE ME A GRATEFUL HEART. YOU MEAN SO MUCH TO ME THAT I WANT TO LEARN MORE ABOUT YOU.

MAKE YOUR HEART A WELCOMING PLACE

Didn't you realize that your body is a sacred place, the place of the Holy Spirit? Don't you see that you can't live however you please, squandering what God paid such a high price for?
1 CORINTHIANS 6:19 MSG

You should feel serious about the body God gave you. Why? His Spirit lives in you. If breaking His rules causes pain, then obeying His instructions makes your heart a welcoming place for His Spirit. God created you, He rescued you, and He gives you everything you need to live. Making your heart, mind, and soul a welcome place for Him is a gift He'd like to receive.

Maybe you didn't know that God's Spirit stays with you always. But *He does*. Have you made Him feel at home? Or do you allow negative feelings or bad choices to diminish your welcoming of God's Spirit? By being careful how you live and keeping your heart clean, you can show Him how much you appreciate His help.

Make your heart an always-welcoming place for God.

I WANT YOU TO FEEL WELCOME, GOD. HELP ME TAKE MY FRIENDSHIP WITH YOU SERIOUSLY SO I CAN ENJOY THE ADVENTURE AND BLESSINGS YOU BRING TO EACH NEW DAY.

SERIOUS GOOD NEWS

Everyone has sinned; we all fall short of God's glorious standard.
ROMANS 3:23 NLT

God's love, grace, and mercy are amazing gifts. But before you can recognize the significance of these gifts, you need to be serious about who you are and who God is. For instance, you can be creative, but God created *everything*. He set the rules for people to live by, but no one keeps them perfectly. You've lived for a few years, but God has lived *forever*.

Does it seem right to think of God as not much different from you? Feeling serious about God means you choose to give Him the honor and respect He deserves.

Yes, God has always loved you—and you've always needed Him. That's *serious* good news. It just makes sense to feel serious about your friendship with God, doesn't it?

I CAN'T DO WHAT YOU CAN DO, LORD. HELP ME TREAT YOU WITH ALL THE HONOR YOU DESERVE. HELP ME REMEMBER THAT GROWING MY FRIENDSHIP WITH YOU IS THE MOST SERIOUS THING I'LL EVER DO.

A GOOD REASON TO THINK ABOUT GOD

These commandments that I give you today are to be on your hearts. Impress them on your children. Talk about them when you sit at home and when you walk along the road, when you lie down and when you get up.

DEUTERONOMY 6:6–7 NIV

Sometimes you'll feel more serious about things like playing sports or video games than you do about getting to know God. You wouldn't be the first person to choose something less important over Him. In the Bible, people had to be reminded that they needed to feel serious about God. They were encouraged to talk about the things God was serious about. What were His rules? Who should follow His rules? These are serious questions you can ask yourself too.

The people were told to think seriously about God all the time—when they talked to their kids, took time to think, relaxed, worked, went to bed, and woke up.

There's always a good reason to think about God and do what He asks.

I'M NOT ALWAYS AS SERIOUS ABOUT YOU AS I SHOULD BE, FATHER. I NEED TO REMEMBER THAT I SHOULD THINK ABOUT YOU THROUGHOUT THE DAY, EVERY DAY OF THE WEEK.

FROM A FROWN TO A SMILE

A glad heart makes a happy face,
but when the heart is sad, the spirit is broken.
PROVERBS 15:13 NLV

Sadness is a feeling you probably wouldn't consider to be good. It can feel kind of like something is broken inside and you want it fixed, right? A lot of feelings are like that.

You've read that God cares enough for you to step in and help. But you can take charge of your feelings too. When you make the *choice* to have a cheerful outlook, you just might discover that the corners of your mouth turn from a frown into a smile.

God invites you to feel cheerful. He knows that whatever you're going through is temporary—it won't last long. When you're cheerful, you're declaring that you trust God and believe that all the bad things going on in your life and in the world will come to an end one day. Will you accept God's invitation to be cheerful?

I KNOW YOU WILL TAKE CARE OF THE FUTURE, GOD. THANK YOU! HELP ME TRUST YOU SO I CAN FEEL CHEERFUL, JOYFUL, AND OPTIMISTIC.

AVOIDING MISERABLE

A miserable heart means a miserable life;
a cheerful heart fills the day with song.
PROVERBS 15:15 MSG

If you're miserable, you feel downright awful. You're unhappy, uncomfortable, unfulfilled. Nothing seems to go right. Everything feels wrong. Being miserable is the last feeling you want to have. When you're sick, you're especially likely to feel miserable. You just want the bad feelings to go away and never come back.

But cheerfulness is a feeling you'd like to keep forever. When you're cheerful, people seem nicer, the day seems brighter, and you look forward to all the new things that could happen.

Sometimes being miserable is out of your control, but other times being miserable is all about the choices you make. You can make choices that get you in trouble, and what comes next (the consequences) makes you feel miserable. Other times, you can feel miserable because someone else made a choice that hurt you.

Choosing to feel cheerful can begin when you notice all the wonderful things God does for you.

I'M GRATEFUL FOR MOMENTS WHEN I FEEL CHEERFUL, LORD. HELP ME REPLACE MY MISERY WITH SOMETHING BETTER. FILL ME WITH YOUR JOY AGAIN.

SHARE GOOD NEWS

A cheerful look brings joy to the heart; good news makes for good health.

PROVERBS 15:30 NLT

You can be a young man who shares the gift of cheerfulness. Do you know how? The happy feeling of cheer can be caught by others when they notice that *you* are cheerful. Cheerfulness is contagious. And when you share good news, others will feel better about the troubles they face.

This is why God doesn't want you to focus your thoughts on all the bad things that could happen. When you do, you'll feel miserable and unhappy, and you'll worry a lot. None of those feelings will help you—and they won't help others either.

You'll never cheer anyone up by choosing to spread misery when you talk with others. It's good to be honest about hard things, but always remember to acknowledge your awesome God who has made good promises and keeps them. Let cheerfulness replace your misery, and then share what you've learned with others.

I DON'T WANT TO MAKE OTHER PEOPLE FEEL MISERABLE, FATHER. HELP ME CHOOSE CHEERFULNESS. I WANT TO DO A GOOD JOB SHARING YOUR GOOD NEWS AND SPREADING CHEER TO OTHERS.

*A cheerful look brings
joy to the heart;
good news makes
for good health.*

GOD WANTS YOUR WORRY

Give all your worries to Him because He cares for you.
1 PETER 5:7 NLV

You might worry about the weather. You might worry about a bully. You might worry about what you'll eat for lunch, what someone might say to you, or whether you'll pass your next test in school.

Worry is a powerful emotion that can also make you feel weak, stressed, and anxious. Worry will never let you be in control (although it makes big promises). Worry can't change the truth. And worry also can't change what *will* happen.

God wants to take away all your feelings of worry. You don't need them, and they don't help anything. God doesn't need them either, and He won't keep them once you give them to Him. After all, God knows everything that will happen, so He never worries. Nothing takes Him by surprise. When you worry, you're telling God that His plan can't be trusted. But it can.

I NEED YOUR HELP SO THAT I DON'T WORRY, LORD. WORRY IS SO MUCH EASIER TO FEEL THAN TRUST. BUT YOUR PLAN FOR ME IS SOMETHING I NEED TO TRUST. . .OR I'LL ALWAYS BE DOUBTING YOUR GOODNESS.

TRUST HIS SOLUTIONS

"Give your entire attention to what God is doing right now, and don't get worked up about what may or may not happen tomorrow. God will help you deal with whatever hard things come up when the time comes."

MATTHEW 6:34 MSG

Do you spend a lot of time doing things that don't help you and aren't necessary? Do you make your bed five times each morning just in case you got it wrong the first time? This is an example of something you might do when you worry. When you worry, you keep thinking about bad things that might never happen, and you allow those things to make you feel sad and frightened.

What if you took some of the time wasted on worry and spent it with God instead? Feeling worried makes it hard to see the good things God is doing. If something bad happens, God can help you get through it. But worrying wastes time and tells God you'd rather spend time thinking about your problems than trusting His solutions.

YOU TAKE CARE OF EVERYTHING, FATHER, SO I NEVER NEED TO WORRY. YOU HAVE A PLAN, AND I'LL NEVER THINK OF ANYTHING BETTER THAN THAT. BECAUSE YOU CARE, I CAN FEEL CALM AND LOVED. THANK YOU.

WORRY NO MORE

"Can all your worries add a single moment to your life?"
MATTHEW 6:27 NLT

If worry could make people live longer, most people would live for a very long time. If worry could make people taller, we'd be living in a land of giants. But worry can't make anyone live longer, and it won't make anyone taller.

Even so, worry can be a pretty powerful emotion. Worry won't help you in any way, but it *can* hurt you. Feeling worried is normal when you don't know God and you aren't sure He can help. You should worry less when you know and trust God. But even then, worry can still hurt you because it distracts you from learning more about God.

It's easy to let your mind think that bad things will happen. When good things happen, you might not fully appreciate those things because you think even good things will lead to bad things. But God tells us that He takes bad things and makes them good.

Praise God!

WORRY SCARES ME, GOD. I OFTEN THINK ABOUT TOO MANY THINGS THAT COULD GO WRONG. HELP ME TO REMEMBER THAT YOU MAKE ALL THINGS RIGHT AND GOOD.

WORRY'S PLAN

"I know the plans I have for you," declares the LORD, *"plans to prosper you and not to harm you, plans to give you hope and a future."*
JEREMIAH 29:11 NIV

If you want to stop feeling worried, then you should change who you listen to. Worry says, "Bad things will happen, and here's a list of everything that could go wrong." But God says, "I have a plan for you, and it's very good." Worry says, "When bad things happen, you'll get hurt." God says, "My plans will not harm you." Worry says, "There's no hope." God says, "I can give you hope and a future."

Who has the most helpful plan? The answer certainly isn't worry! God has a plan that will *always* help you.

WORRY CAN'T HELP ME FEEL BRAVE, LORD. WORRY DOESN'T WANT ME TO REMEMBER THAT YOU'RE GOOD AND YOUR PLANS ARE AWESOME. HELP ME REFUSE TO LISTEN TO WORRY.

BRAVERY: THE WORRY BUSTER

God did not give us a spirit of fear. He gave us a spirit of power and of love and of a good mind.
2 TIMOTHY 1:7 NLV

Bravery is one of the things God uses to help His people combat worry. Where worry believes everything that can go wrong will go wrong, bravery willingly stands up and says, "I will face any trouble, now or in the future, with my best friend, God!"

God doesn't give instructions on good ways to worry. Instead, He wants you to know that worry doesn't come from Him—not ever! God says that He gives you the strength you need, the love others need, and a good mind to help you remember His good gifts.

Feel brave today because God says you should. Feel strong because God gives you strength. Feel love because it's God's greatest rule. Bravery doesn't mean you think you're strong enough to do things on your own—it just means you know the God who *is* strong enough to do even the impossible.

MAKE ME BRAVE, FATHER. MAKE ME STRONG AND WISE. HELP ME SAY GOODBYE TO THE FEELING OF WORRY BECAUSE YOU ALWAYS WALK WITH ME—AND YOU'LL MAKE SURE I NEVER GET LOST.

BRAVE ENOUGH TO TRY

I was unsure of how to go about this, and felt totally inadequate—I was scared to death, if you want the truth of it—and so nothing I said could have impressed you or anyone else.
1 CORINTHIANS 2:3 MSG

The apostle Paul went through all kinds of trouble. God used him to write many of the books in the New Testament. When worry kept trying to take over, Paul chose to feel brave. He didn't feel he was the best person to share God's message; in fact, he thought he was weak and had nothing to offer. He admitted he was scared. Paul thought that nothing he said would impress the people who might listen to him.

When you're full of doubt like Paul, recognize that this is when you need bravery the most. Eventually, God will ask you to do something you aren't sure you can do. You could say no to every new adventure—or, because God is the one asking, you can bravely say, "I can't. . .but with You, all things are possible."

EVERYTHING I'VE EVER DONE STARTED WITH A YES, GOD. WHEN YOU HAVE SOMETHING NEW FOR ME TO DO, HELP ME REMEMBER THAT WITH YOU BY MY SIDE I CAN BE BRAVE ENOUGH TO TRY.

Face Trouble Bravely

The wicked run away when no one is chasing them, but the godly are as bold as lions.
PROVERBS 28:1 NLT

It's hard to feel brave when you're all alone. When you don't know God, it's easy to feel worried because deep down you're unsure whether you can handle everything life throws your way. You feel like you don't know how to face anything bravely—in fact, you don't want to face trouble at all. People who don't know God will run away from trouble because they feel defeated before they even try.

But when you *do* know God—and you *do* walk with Him—bravery is possible. After all, you know the God who made everything and who rescues people like you. He never hides from people who are brave enough to seek Him.

Don't allow worry or fear to steal your hope. *Be brave.* It will make your life so much better, and others will be encouraged too.

HELP ME BE BRAVE, LORD. I WANT TO FEEL CLOSE TO YOU SO I CAN BE CERTAIN I'LL NEVER HAVE TO FACE ANYTHING ALONE.

Yes, Even When. . .

"I am the LORD your God who takes hold of your right hand and says to you, Do not fear; I will help you."
ISAIAH 41:13 NIV

You should feel brave when you follow God. There's no reason not to feel brave. Even when you don't have the answers, God does. Even when you might be afraid, God never is. Even when you'd rather say no, the truth is that God is looking for someone like you who's willing to do His work. When you say yes to God, your feelings of bravery will include trust and confidence. Each new adventure with God should be easier because you've seen how He works and helps you do amazing things.

Like an adult who holds your hand when you're learning to walk, God walks with you and tells you everything will be all right because He's there to help you. Your trust in God is just what you need to be brave!

I DON'T WANT TO PRETEND TO BE BRAVE, FATHER. I WANT TO KNOW FOR SURE THAT YOU'LL HELP ME AND THAT I CAN TRUST YOU. WITH YOU, I REALLY CAN BE BRAVE.

Value others above yourselves, not looking to your own interests but each of you to the interests of the others.

EVERYONE HAS DREAMS AND PLANS

Value others above yourselves, not looking to your own interests but each of you to the interests of the others.
PHILIPPIANS 2:3–4 NIV

It's common for boys your age to compare themselves with others. If you think someone is better than you, then you also feel like you're *not as good* as they are. They might be better at sports or video games or be more popular. On the flip side, you might think some people aren't as good as you are. When you compare, you'll always think of some people as better and others as worse. Thankfully, that's not the way God looks at people. And He wants to change the way you think.

If you can get past the feeling of being unconcerned, then you can begin to recognize that everyone has dreams and plans—just like you. You'll look for ways to encourage or help them. Pay attention to the things others are interested in, and reach out to help them when you believe God is nudging you to help.

I ALWAYS FEEL BETTER ABOUT MYSELF WHEN I ENCOURAGE OTHERS, GOD. I CAN LEARN SO MUCH FROM YOU AS I CHANGE THE WAY I THINK AND BEGIN TO MAKE BETTER CHOICES.

NOT THAT CONCERNED

Do not keep good from those who should have it, when it is in your power to do it.
PROVERBS 3:27 NLV

Have you ever felt concerned? It's probably true that you care about a few things, but if you're honest, most of the things you care about have to do with *you*. . .right?

You could make the choice to do good things that would help other people, but you're just not sure you're *that* concerned about *their* problems. You might think their struggles are their own fault and have zilch to do with you.

Job was a man in the Bible (you read about him earlier in this book) who went through some very hard things. He could have used some good friends to help him through a very difficult time, but three men who called themselves "friends" showed up and decided they weren't all that concerned. They kept accusing Job of things he hadn't even done. They chose not to encourage him. Job needed support from his friends, but they chose to pile on the blame instead. Unconcern makes life harder for others. Step in and help where and when you can. Ask God to show you what you can do.

I DON'T WANT TO FEEL UNCONCERNED, GOD. YOU CARE ABOUT ME. HELP ME CARE ABOUT OTHERS.

ACTUAL HELP

Suppose you see a brother or sister who has no food or clothing, and you say, "Good-bye and have a good day; stay warm and eat well"— but then you don't give that person any food or clothing. What good does that do?

JAMES 2:15–16 NLT

God is kind, and He will help if you'll let Him. He doesn't have feelings of unconcern for you. He wants something much better for you, and He's ready to do what you can't do on your own to help you get there.

The book of James shows the way some people act when they see a person in need. Some people who claim to follow God will say nice words, but they won't *do* anything to help. They don't spring into action.

It can be hard to know what to do when you think that someone doesn't really need the help or that they might not be telling you the truth. But you can always ask God for guidance so you can help in the right way.

WHEN I SEE A NEED, LORD, HELP ME TO DO MORE THAN SAY NICE THINGS. HELP ME TO ACT! SHOW ME WHAT TO DO.

Concern versus Worry

Love takes everything that comes without giving up. Love believes all things. Love hopes for all things. Love keeps on in all things.
1 CORINTHIANS 13:7 NLV

Feeling concerned might sound a little like feeling worried, but that's not necessarily true. When you feel worried, you can't control what you're worried about. When you feel concerned, you're led to make better choices and set clearer priorities.

If you're concerned about your friendship with God, then you can choose to read more about Him and talk to Him in prayer. If you're concerned about a friend, then you can choose to help him. If you're concerned about what a friend may be doing, you can choose to pray for him and talk to him.

Worry usually doesn't lead to helpful choices in life. But being concerned means you're willing to make choices and take actions that are helpful to others.

Being concerned may mean refusing to give up on anyone and believing in others and hoping for good things in their lives.

WHEN I'M CONCERNED, LET ME NOT FEEL WORRIED TOO, LORD. I WANT TO CARE FOR OTHERS BY MAKING THE GOOD CHOICE TO HELP.

LOOKING FOR RESULTS

The earnest prayer of a righteous person has great power and produces wonderful results.

JAMES 5:16 NLT

While the feeling of worry leaves you thinking, *I don't know what to do*, concern will tell you that you *can* do something. Start with prayer and ask God to help you know what to do next. James 5 says if you make the choice to pray and don't give up, then you shouldn't be surprised when your concern changes things for the person you're concerned about.

Worry tells God that you don't think He can help. But concern gives you the opportunity to ask Him for the help you *believe* He can give. If you're worried but instead say you're concerned, then you might want to rethink what you believe is true about God. He can take your worries and concerns and do something about them.

If you're concerned and looking for results, pray.

YOU WANT ME TO BE CONCERNED ENOUGH TO PRAY, FATHER. YOU DON'T WANT ME TO FEEL WORRIED AND THEN NEVER DO ANYTHING ABOUT IT.

SPIRITUAL FITNESS

Stay clear of silly stories that get dressed up as religion. Exercise daily in God—no spiritual flabbiness, please! Workouts in the gymnasium are useful, but a disciplined life in God is far more so, making you fit both today and forever. You can count on this.

1 TIMOTHY 4:7–8 MSG

People are pretty good at making things up. They tell stories that might sound true, but actually they're nothing more than make-believe stories. They might even tell you things about God that aren't true. God says you should stay away from these silly stories. The best way to do that is to keep learning more about what God's Word really says and spending time with Him every day.

You might think that spending time at the gym is a great idea, but when the gym becomes more important than God, then you become weak spiritually. When you don't make an intentional choice to follow God, it's much easier to believe those untrue stories.

I WANT TO BE SPIRITUALLY FIT, GOD. HELP ME TO BE CONCERNED ENOUGH THAT I MAKE CHOICES THAT BRING ME CLOSER TO YOU.

GO BEYOND WORDS

Let us not love with words or speech
but with actions and in truth.
1 JOHN 3:18 NIV

When you feel concerned about others, it's the perfect time to *do* something about how you feel. You might remember that love is more than just a feeling—it's an action. So when you love others, you do things to show how much you care.

If all you say to members of your family is, "I love you," but you don't do anything to show that love, then you need to do more. Go beyond words and really love others in both your words *and* your actions. Take all the things God teaches you into consideration, because that information will affect what you say and what you believe to be true about God and His love.

Concern can be the starting point to feelings of compassion, love, and kindness.

I DON'T JUST WANT TO SAY, "I LOVE YOU," LORD.
LET ME SHOW MY LOVE THROUGH MY ACTIONS
SO OTHERS CAN SEE IT AND FEEL IT.

YOUR OWN BOSS

A time is coming when people will no longer listen to sound and wholesome teaching. They will follow their own desires and will look for teachers who will tell them whatever their itching ears want to hear.
2 TIMOTHY 4:3 NLT

A lot of people want to believe that whatever they do is okay. They don't want anyone to tell them they shouldn't. They'll keep looking for someone to say that their wrong choice is good. And at some point, they'll probably find a person who agrees with them. Then they'll treat this wrong information as if everyone should agree.

God knew this feeling would exist. He knew people would want someone to tell them that their bad choices are actually good choices. If this sounds like you, then you are following something besides God. Maybe you want to be your own boss instead of following God's rules. But know that when God tells you the truth, it's never to make you feel uncomfortable—it's to help you stay away from hurt.

IF I TRY TO BE MY OWN BOSS, I'LL MAKE A LOT OF BAD DECISIONS, GOD. KEEP ME FROM BELIEVING FAKE STORIES WHEN YOU ALWAYS TELL THE TRUTH.

WHEN GOD TELLS YOU THE TRUTH, IT'S NEVER TO MAKE YOU FEEL UNCOMFORTABLE— IT'S TO HELP YOU STAY AWAY FROM HURT.

Where Every Step Is Troubled

So watch your step. Use your head. Make the most of every chance you get. These are desperate times!
EPHESIANS 5:15–16 MSG

Feeling as though you don't need to follow God is dangerous because there's always the question of who you're following. If you're not following God, are you better off than if you were following Him? Be careful where you walk, who you walk with, and what you think.

You have a chance to share what you're learning with others who also need to choose who to follow. Since life is full of twists and turns, it's always best to choose your leader (God!), follow Him faithfully, and let others know why this is an amazing choice.

You could choose instead to walk away to a place where every step leads to trouble, your thinking is confused, and your time is wasted on things that aren't very important. When you consider the different paths you could take in life, you have a few things to think about that may help make your choice of who to follow a little easier.

THERE'S MORE THAN ONE PATH I COULD TAKE, LORD. PLEASE GIVE ME THE WISDOM TO MAKE THE ONGOING DECISION TO FOLLOW YOU.

THE MESSAGE DELIVERER

Jonah ran away from the LORD and headed for Tarshish. He went down to Joppa, where he found a ship bound for that port. After paying the fare, he went aboard and sailed for Tarshish to flee from the LORD.

JONAH 1:3 NIV

The story of Jonah shows what it's like to walk away from God. When Jonah walked away, it wasn't because he didn't know God. In fact, God called Jonah a prophet. He delivered messages for God. But when Jonah received a new message that he didn't like, he decided to walk away from God.

Actually, Jonah didn't just walk away; he decided to "flee [run] from the LORD." Jonah wanted out, but God cared enough to remind Jonah of why he followed God in the first place. God is good, kind, and full of mercy!

When Jonah ran away, he lived through a storm at sea and three nights in the belly of a big fish. When he walked with God once more, he had a wonderful message to share with others.

HELP ME SEE HOW IMPORTANT IT IS TO BE CAREFUL WHO I FOLLOW, FATHER. HELP ME RUN AWAY FROM ANYONE AND ANYTHING THAT ISN'T YOU.

CREATED FOR FRIENDSHIP

The Lord God called to the man.
He said to him, "Where are you?"
GENESIS 3:9 NLV

God wants you to follow Him. He really does. We follow Him when we obey Him and do what His Word tells us to do. But maybe you're curious and tempted to do the opposite of what God says. Sin can—and will—stop you from following Him. It might even cause you to try to hide from God. This is what happened with the first man and woman. Adam and Eve broke the only rule God had given them. As a result, instead of looking forward to their time with God, they avoided Him.

You were created for friendship with God—just like Adam and Eve. These two thought they could hide from Him, but God knows everything. And even though He knew where they were, God called out, "Where are you?" He wanted the two people who broke His rule to come to Him. They finally did, but they regretted not listening to God.

The longer you follow God, the easier it gets to make the choice to listen to Him. If you ever fail, God will give you a do-over. Make the good choice to follow Him once more.

I WANT YOU AS MY VERY BEST FRIEND, GOD.
I DON'T WANT TO BE AFRAID TO TELL YOU ANYTHING.
GIVE ME A DEEP DESIRE TO FOLLOW YOU.

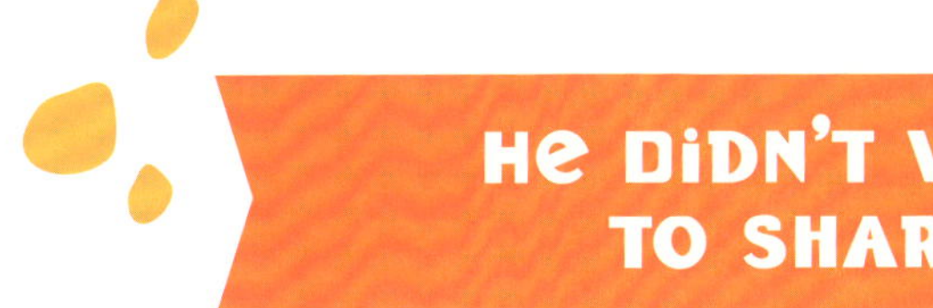

HE DIDN'T WANT TO SHARE

"You must love the LORD your God with all your heart, all your soul, all your strength, and all your mind."
LUKE 10:27 NLT

The man speaking to Jesus was rich. He had also been pretty good at following God, but maybe he just wasn't feeling it that day. Jesus asked him to explain what he needed to do to be rescued, and the man actually gave a very good answer. He said that people should love God with everything they had and then love everyone else (sound familiar?).

But Jesus knew the part of the answer that the man refused to say. He didn't love God or people more than he loved his money. When the man wanted to know what else he could do, Jesus told him to use his wealth to help people. But sadly, the man didn't want to share his wealth with anyone else.

When you truly want to follow God, nothing should be more important than doing what He asks you to do.

INSPIRE ME TO FOLLOW YOU, LORD. WHEN YOU HAVE SOMETHING FOR ME TO DO, HELP ME NOT TO MAKE ANY EXCUSES.

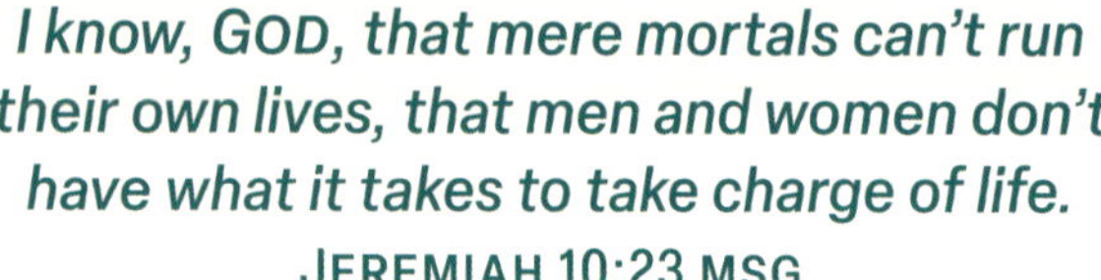

WHO'S INSPIRING YOUR CHOICES

I know, GOD, that mere mortals can't run their own lives, that men and women don't have what it takes to take charge of life.
JEREMIAH 10:23 MSG

Jeremiah was one of God's messengers, or prophets, and he had a message to share. Jeremiah had observed a lot of people. He saw that the people's bad choices led to more bad choices. . .and there was a big difference between what God had asked them to do and what they were actually doing.

Jeremiah learned that people aren't very good at running their own lives. No one can make perfect decisions about what to do with their life.

Following God is what people should be doing, but so many refuse to walk with Him. Sadly, many people are willing to walk toward anything other than God.

God inspires good choices that lead to good feelings. But people are often inspired by lies and feelings that lead them to believe that God isn't very important. Who or what is inspiring your choices?

KEEP ENCOURAGING ME TO OBEY, FATHER. I WANT TO WALK WITH YOU, TALK WITH YOU, AND LEARN FROM YOU. I DON'T WANT TO WALK AWAY.

THE ENEMY

"The thief comes only to steal and kill and destroy; I have come that they may have life, and have it to the full."
JOHN 10:10 NIV

God's enemy is sometimes referred to as a thief. He will take almost anything you're willing to give him. He'll take your time, attention, loyalty, and interests. Anytime this thief can keep you from following God, he is pleased.

He doesn't want you to succeed. He doesn't want you to feel satisfied. He absolutely hates it when you follow God. He knows God sent Jesus to give you life—and this is a life God's enemy doesn't want you to have.

You have the choice to follow the God who leads you into new adventures, or to follow His enemy, who only wants to see you lose.

Who do you feel like following today? Why?

HELP ME BELIEVE THAT YOU ALONE HAVE MY BEST INTERESTS IN MIND, GOD. MAKE ME CAUTIOUS ABOUT LISTENING TO OTHERS WHEN I SHOULD BE FOLLOWING YOU INSTEAD.

GOD IS GOING PLACES.
ARE YOU FOLLOWING HIM
OR FALLING BEHIND?

FOLLOWING GOD'S WORD

All Scripture is inspired by God and is useful to teach us what is true and to make us realize what is wrong in our lives. It corrects us when we are wrong and teaches us to do what is right.

2 TIMOTHY 3:16 NLT

What comes to mind when you think about the Bible? Is the Bible just a good place to read words that make you feel good about God? Is it a book you keep on your shelf because it seems important to have it around?

It's so much more than that! God spoke the words you read in the Bible. His Word is the way He talks to you, teaches you, and helps you make good choices. The Bible speaks the truth and helps you understand the difference between what's right and what's wrong, between what's worth doing and what should be avoided.

When you read one of God's instructions in the Bible and it's the opposite of how you normally do things, it's important to adjust your feelings and choices to match what God's Word says.

MY CHOICES ARE IMPORTANT TO YOU, FATHER. HELP ME KNOW THE DIFFERENCE BETWEEN FOLLOWING YOUR WORD AND NOT FOLLOWING YOUR WORD. MY FEELINGS ARE HAPPIER WHEN I FOLLOW THE TEACHINGS OF THE BIBLE.

NEVER PUSHED PAST YOUR LIMIT

No test or temptation that comes your way is beyond the course of what others have had to face. All you need to remember is that God will never let you down; he'll never let you be pushed past your limit; he'll always be there to help you come through it.

1 CORINTHIANS 10:13 MSG

If you're in the middle of a struggle that makes you feel uncomfortable, then God has some good news, and it involves a choice *He* makes. When you feel stressed and unsettled, God thinks about the choice that He made long before you were born—*He won't let you down*. He'll stop your struggle before it becomes too much. He'll help you move past all the uneasy feelings.

God doesn't promise that you'll never feel uncomfortable. But when you follow God, there's a limit to how uncomfortable He'll allow you to feel. Of course, you have a responsibility too: Your part is to pray and rely on God and accept His help.

I DON'T LIKE FEELING UNCOMFORTABLE, GOD. I FEEL LIKE ONE STEP IN THE WRONG DIRECTION WOULD BE A DISASTER. HELP ME MOVE ON TO BETTER, HAPPIER, MORE COMFORTABLE FEELINGS.

LEARNING TO TRUST

We also glory in our sufferings, because we know that suffering produces perseverance; perseverance, character; and character, hope. And hope does not put us to shame, because God's love has been poured out into our hearts through the Holy Spirit, who has been given to us.

ROMANS 5:3–5 NIV

Feeling uncomfortable isn't all bad. You learn more about yourself when you face uncomfortable moments. You learn how dependable God is in those moments too. Romans 5 describes a way to move from feeling uncomfortable to hopeful. It starts with suffering, then transitions to patience, improved personal character, and hope.

Because God continually fills you with His love, you are able to move away from uncomfortable feelings. His love overflows until it spills onto others and leads them toward hope too.

Feeling uncomfortable probably isn't a place you want to be, but God can use it for good to build your trust in Him.

WHEN I FEEL UNCOMFORTABLE, HELP ME LEARN TO TRUST YOU EVEN MORE, LORD. I WANT THIS NEGATIVE FEELING TO LEAD ME TO WELCOME YOUR HELP.

STiCK WiTH GOD

You belong to God, my dear children. You have already won a victory over those people, because the Spirit who lives in you is greater than the spirit who lives in the world.

1 JOHN 4:4 NLT

There may be times when you feel uncomfortable, and it isn't a test to help you grow in your faith. No, this kind of *uncomfortable* is introduced by God's enemy, and he uses it to try to get you to stop following God. Fight against this feeling.

Stick with God. He has already won the victory over evil. He's greater, stronger, and wiser than His enemy—or anyone else for that matter. Feeling uncomfortable when the enemy is trying to sway your heart is a good thing, because it means you're learning more about God. And when you feel uncomfortable around lies, it means you're learning the truth. Anytime you feel confused, God's Spirit can help you recognize the difference between what is true and what's not. Just say a prayer and see what He says to your heart.

I NEED YOU, FATHER. I DON'T LIKE FEELING CONFUSED AND UNCOMFORTABLE. I TRUST YOU TO PROVIDE THE COMFORT I NEED.

Keep Reminding Yourself

He answered me, "I am all you need. I give you My loving-favor. My power works best in weak people." I am happy to be weak and have troubles so I can have Christ's power in me. I receive joy when I am weak. I receive joy when people talk against me and make it hard for me and try to hurt me and make trouble for me. I receive joy when all these things come to me because of Christ. For when I am weak, then I am strong.

2 CORINTHIANS 12:9–10 NLV

Weakness will make you feel uncomfortable. It will make you feel helpless. But you can rest assured that you're never without comfort or help from God. His Spirit will work within you to get rid of those uncomfortable feelings in your heart. He gives help to those who need it. He gives strength to those who feel weak.

Second Corinthians 12:9–10 talks about the apostle Paul's many feelings. Paul reminded himself that God always showed up when bad feelings threatened to lead him to do the wrong thing.

I NEED TO BE REMINDED, GOD, THAT YOU NEVER WANT ME TO BE UNCOMFORTABLE AND STAY THAT WAY. WHEN YOU HELP ME, MY FEELINGS CHANGE FOR THE BETTER.

A Better Tomorrow

At day's end I'm ready for sound sleep,
for you, GOD, have put my life back together.
PSALM 4:8 MSG

Many people believe that King David wrote the words of Psalm 4. There were many times when David felt uncomfortable. Difficult days were normal for the king. Verse 8 shows us David's thoughts after the stress and worry of an uncomfortable moment in his life.

If David's life was like a broken ceramic mug, then the words of this psalm express his gratitude that God had taken all the bits and pieces and glued them back together as good as new. This gift from God gave David the feeling of being relaxed and at ease. With God in our lives, there's no such thing as a worst-case scenario. When we let Him, He'll turn all bad days into better tomorrows.

WHEN I FEEL BROKEN, LORD, PIECE ME BACK TOGETHER SO I CAN RELAX AND FEEL AT EASE. THANK YOU FOR ALWAYS WANTING TO HELP ME HEAL FROM THE HARD THINGS.

WHEN I BECOME STRONGER

I know what it is to be in need, and I know what it is to have plenty. I have learned the secret of being content in any and every situation, whether well fed or hungry, whether living in plenty or in want. I can do all this through him who gives me strength.

PHILIPPIANS 4:12–13 NIV

It's easier to feel relaxed when you're not worried about anything. Sure, your life isn't perfect, but you can relax knowing God is taking care of literally everything.

The apostle Paul had needs he couldn't take care of on his own. He needed food and didn't have it. He even had a few things he wanted and couldn't get. But Paul didn't throw a pity party. No. Instead, he said something unexpected. Paul essentially said, "I've experienced the good and the bad, but when I remember that God is the one who takes care of me, I can relax. That's when I become stronger."

THERE'S NO GOOD REASON TO BE UNCOMFORTABLE WHEN I'M WITH YOU, FATHER. GIVE ME THE COURAGE TO TRUST THAT NO MATTER WHAT I FACE, YOU'RE IN CONTROL.

A GOOD REASON TO RELAX

Jesus said to His followers, "Because of this, I say to you, do not worry about your life, what you are going to eat. Do not worry about your body, what you are going to wear. Life is worth more than food. The body is worth more than clothes."
LUKE 12:22–23 NLV

Here in Luke 12, Jesus was talking to His disciples. It seems there were two things they kept thinking about. They wanted to know when and what they'd eat, and they were curious about what clothing they'd have access to.

They weren't feeling very relaxed. They were worried. Jesus told them it was time to stop. . .and trust. Their life was possible because God took care of everything. God provided air and water. But He also provided love, acceptance, and forgiveness. Jesus asked those who were listening to open their eyes a little wider and see all the blessings God provided so they could really live. Maybe His reassuring words will give you a good reason to relax too.

I DON'T KNOW WHY I DON'T FEEL MORE RELAXED, GOD. YOU ALWAYS TAKE CARE OF ME. HELP ME REMEMBER TO THANK YOU FOR YOUR PERFECT GIFTS.

DECISIONS MADE IN GOD'S DIRECTION

"Seek the Kingdom of God above all else, and live righteously, and he will give you everything you need."
MATTHEW 6:33 NLT

You feel relaxed when you know that what you're looking for is worth finding. . .when what you're living for is to follow God. . .when what you need is also what you want.

Nothing will ever be better than chasing after God. He's worth knowing, talking to, and walking beside. He has a plan, and He wants you to follow it because He knows that no other plan is better for you.

You'll feel satisfied, content, and relaxed when you choose to chase after Him. But just thinking about your friendship with Him on Sundays at church isn't enough. Wouldn't it be a good idea to spend more time—every day—with the God who will help you relax?

MAY MY QUEST TO FOLLOW YOU BE A DAILY PRIORITY, LORD. I FEEL RELAXED WHEN I'M WITH YOU BECAUSE I KNOW YOU LOVE ME.

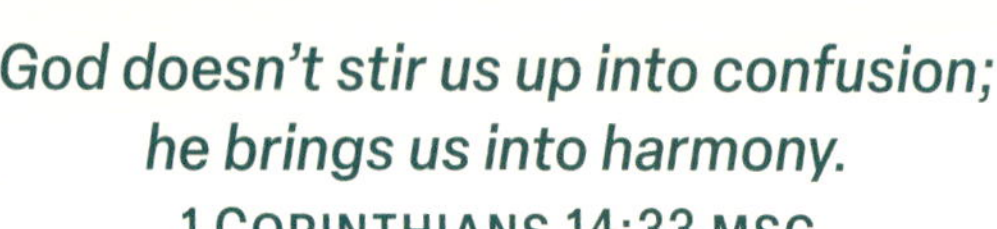

NO NEED TO FEEL CONFUSED

God doesn't stir us up into confusion;
he brings us into harmony.
1 CORINTHIANS 14:33 MSG

It's no fun feeling confused. When you're unsure, it's hard to make any choice—let alone a good one. Confusion leaves you guessing and then guessing again. You're not sure you can even tell right from wrong. You're no longer certain how you should respond to others. All kinds of feelings bubble up in your heart, but none of them seem helpful. You might feel frustration, impatience, or even anger, but nothing you think of seems like the right thing to do.

God doesn't want your thoughts to be in turmoil, so He has given you His Word and His Spirit to teach you what you should do. With God's wisdom, there's no need to feel confused.

God can help you make sense of your jumbled feelings. You don't have to live without knowing which way to go or what choice to make. God will *always* lead you to what's best.

I DON'T LIKE CHAOS, FATHER. AND WITH YOUR HELP, I CAN AVOID IT. WITH YOUR WISDOM, I CAN DISCOVER PEACE.

God doesn't stir us up into confusion; he brings us into harmony.

THE CHAOS OF BROKEN WALLS

A person without self-control is like a city with broken-down walls.
PROVERBS 25:28 NLT

Once upon a time, most cities had walls surrounding them. These walls protected the people by keeping away outsiders who wanted to steal from the people and hurt them during a time when darkness made it easy for outsiders to get in and create trouble.

Self-control is like those city walls. It offers protection from chaos that could be harmful to you. When you can't control your own actions, you create chaos for yourself and others. It's like choosing to break down walls that were built to protect.

The good news is that God can help you control your actions, decisions, and choices. Self-control is simply working with God to create a life dedicated to reducing and getting rid of chaos.

I WANT TO COOPERATE WITH YOU, LORD. YOU HAVE THE BEST SOLUTIONS, BUT THEY WON'T HELP ME IF I DON'T TRUST YOU TO LEAD ME AWAY FROM THE CHAOS.

CONTAGIOUS CONFUSION

A nation falls where there is no wise leading, but it is safe where there are many wise men who know what to do.
PROVERBS 11:14 NLV

The feelings of confusion and chaos can be contagious. Similar to catching a cold, these two feelings can infect anyone who's near with fear, worry, and discontent. And like a cold, these bad feelings can keep spreading from person to person with no end in sight. This cycle leads to even more feelings of sadness, nervousness, and depression.

But Proverbs 11:14 says there's a group of people who welcome God's wisdom when they need to make decisions. They know that God is good and always will be good. These people trust in God and seek His answers so they can avoid chaos. You can feel safe and assured when you spend time with people who avoid chaos by following God.

HELP ME CHOOSE FRIENDS WHO FOLLOW YOU, FATHER. I DON'T WANT CONFUSION TO BE MY NORMAL WAY OF DEALING WITH THINGS. YOU HAVE SOMETHING MUCH BETTER IN STORE FOR ME.

THE MASTER OF PEACE

May the Master of Peace himself give you the gift of getting along with each other at all times, in all ways. May the Master be truly among you!
2 THESSALONIANS 3:16 MSG

Do you have any brothers or sisters? If so, is it easy to get along with them, to feel peace? Or do you usually have chaos in your home?

The apostle Paul referred to Jesus as the "Master of Peace." Paul prayed to the God of peace because he wanted to give the people the gift of getting along. Sounds wonderful, doesn't it? Imagine what it would be like to get along with everyone in your home. Imagine how great it would be to avoid chaos at school or when you play sports or video games.

No one needs chaos. But everyone needs peace. You can feel at peace when you recognize God's gift, accept it, and discover that getting along brings calm.

IF GETTING ALONG WITH OTHERS IS A GIFT, THEN I WANT IT, GOD. I OFFICIALLY PUT PEACE ON MY WISH LIST. WOULD YOU HELP ME FIND IT?

HE MAKES THINGS GOOD

You will keep in perfect peace those whose minds are steadfast, because they trust in you.
ISAIAH 26:3 NIV

When your life feels chaotic, it could be because you have stopped seeking God. You don't pray, don't read the Bible, and don't think about what you've learned about God.

If you wonder why you feel peace when you pay attention to God, it has to do with the change that happens inside when you trust Him. When He becomes more to you than a character in a big book or someone you spend time with only on the weekends, you can *really* get to know Him. And when you know Him, you can begin to trust that God always makes things good.

No matter what kind of problems you have, things will always go better when you pay attention to God, trust Him, and discover the feeling of peace that He brings. The best choice you can make to enjoy this kind of peace is to put your trust in God.

THE FEELING OF PEACE ISN'T SOMETHING I CAN FIND JUST ANYWHERE, LORD. LET MY EYES FOCUS ON YOU, LET MY MIND LEARN FROM YOU, AND LET MY HEART FEEL YOUR PEACE.

CHERISH IT WHEN YOU FIND IT

The Lord said, "I Myself will go with you. I will give you rest."
EXODUS 33:14 NLV

This verse in Exodus 33 talks about the peace you feel when you get a good rest. God promises to be with you—so you can worry less and rest more! God wants you (and He wanted the Israelites in Exodus) to know that He walks with you, and He assures you that you never need to feel overwhelmed. He will help you. He doesn't want you to experience chaos—but He does want you to feel peace.

Have you ever sighed when you were thinking of something that made you feel happy or content? Maybe you can remember a time when you gazed at the twinkling stars, a beautiful mountain, or a powerful waterfall. That memory may have even brought a smile to your face just now. Feelings of awe often come from the same place as the peace you feel. Ask God to help you find peace—and then thank Him when you find it.

PEACE IS SUCH A WONDERFUL FEELING, FATHER.
I WANT TO EXPERIENCE THIS FEELING MORE OFTEN.
WILL YOU PLEASE SHOW ME WHERE TO FIND IT?

THE PEACE FLIGHT

"Who will give me wings," I ask—"wings like a dove?" Get me out of here on dove wings; I want some peace and quiet. I want a walk in the country, I want a cabin in the woods. I'm desperate for a change from rage and stormy weather.

PSALM 55:6–8 MSG

Adults might take vacations or days off from work to help them relax after especially busy, challenging, or overwhelming periods. They would agree that the feeling of peace is worth pursuing. King David talked about this in Psalm 55. He was so fed up with being busy that he said he wished he had wings. Because if he had wings, he could fly away to a place where he could feel at peace. Today we might try to find peace when we go for a walk in the woods or spend a few days at a remote mountain cabin. David felt like he lived in a storm, and all he really wanted was the feeling of peace.

Pursue the feeling of peace—it's worth it! Ask God to help. Then receive and rejoice.

PEACE IS SOMETHING I WANT, GOD. REMOVE THE NEGATIVE FEELINGS THAT PREVENT ME FROM EXPERIENCING YOUR PEACE, AND KEEP ME CALM WHILE I WAIT.

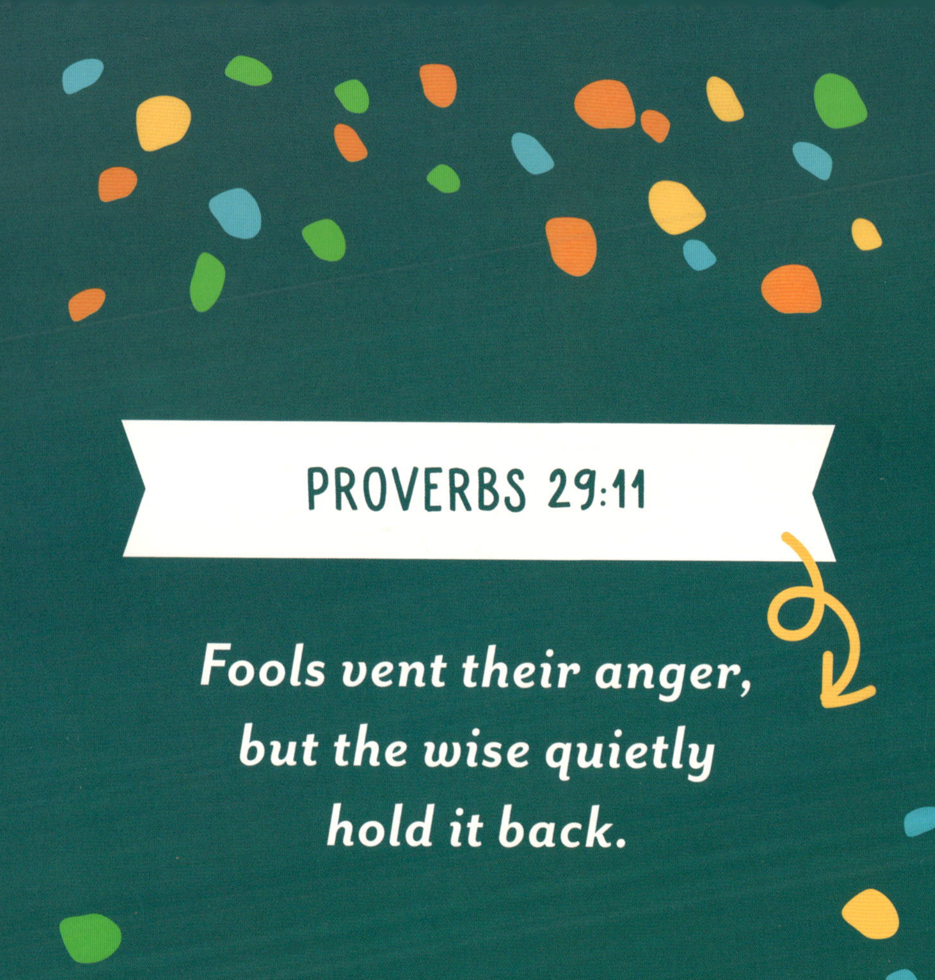

PROVERBS 29:11

Fools vent their anger, but the wise quietly hold it back.

A FOOLiSH CHOiCe

Fools vent their anger,
but the wise quietly hold it back.
PROVERBS 29:11 NLT

You might get angry and say whatever comes to mind, but it's usually better to keep your thoughts to yourself for a while. When you think about your words before speaking them, you'll rarely regret it.

A scientific study shows that if you can take a time-out from expressing angry or negative feelings, you just might change your attitude. But you can bet this study was no surprise to God. He knew that feeling angry and acting rude would be a common reaction when people say or do things we don't like. But God said that it's foolish to use our words to spread anger. He also said it's wise to think first about what you could or should say.

Sometimes it takes time for us to discover what God already knows—making rude comments based on angry feelings is a very foolish choice.

HELP ME BE CAREFUL WITH MY WORDS WHEN I FEEL LIKE BEING RUDE, LORD. WILL MY WORDS HELP SOMEONE? IF NOT, MAYBE I SHOULD LET YOU HELP THEM—AND THEN ME.

The Quilt of Love

Hatred starts fights, but love pulls a quilt over the bickering.
PROVERBS 10:12 MSG

A fire needs oxygen to keep burning. When a fire is small enough, some firefighters might recommend using a cloth to cover and smother the flame. This stops the fire by making sure no extra oxygen gets to it. Without oxygen, the flames can't continue to burn.

Hatred, anger, and rude words start fights (like the flames of a fire), but love covers up the damage of rude words (like a cloth that smothers and puts out the fire). If you wait too long to address an issue, you'll need to make a lot of repairs to fix the damage caused by an argument. So it's always best to choose love over anger and rudeness.

If you don't like fights (and you shouldn't), then do what you can to remove the heat of rudeness. This choice may be difficult when you're angry, but it's yours to make.

YOU HAVE A GREAT WAY WITH WORDS, GOD. THANK YOU FOR HELPING ME UNDERSTAND THAT I CAN PUT AN END TO ARGUMENTS WITH YOUR QUILT OF LOVE.

GOOD WORDS

Watch your talk! No bad words should be coming from your mouth. Say what is good. Your words should help others grow as Christians.

EPHESIANS 4:29 NLV

God says that He has expectations for those who follow Him. You should love others, forgive them, show kindness, and be careful about the words you speak. The list goes on, but pay special attention to the last one mentioned in verse 29—*be careful about the words you use.*

You represent God. What people hear you say will affect how they think and feel about God. If you say you love God but are rude, then others will wonder if God is rude too. The words you use and the way you use them are important. You should speak only good, kind, and loving words. Ephesians 4:29 (NLV) says, "Your words should help others grow as Christians." Do your words do that? If you're not sure, ask God to help you change your words so you use them only for good.

USING ONLY GOOD WORDS MEANS I'LL HAVE TO THINK MORE, LORD. I NEED TO ASK YOU FOR HELP IN CHOOSING GOOD WORDS. I PRAY THAT WHAT I SAY HELPS OTHERS.

DON'T TRY TO TAKE GOD'S JOB

Since we are receiving a Kingdom that is unshakable, let us be thankful and please God by worshiping him with holy fear and awe.

HEBREWS 12:28 NLT

You've learned that rudeness should never be your first response to others. If you spend too much time focusing on what other people do or don't do, then you might be trying to take God's job. He does things perfectly, and He knows everything. So if someone is rude to you, He knows it—you don't have to tell Him.

God promised those who follow Him a forever home in heaven. Someday you won't think about who was rude to you, who you were angry with, or even how sad you were, because you get to be with God *forever*! When that day comes, all the things that were once wrong in the world will never be a problem again. Feel thankfulness in your heart today. You can invite praise and awe too. Today's bad feelings will end. God's future won't. Look forward to that!

EVEN WHEN I'M UNHAPPY ABOUT WHAT HAPPENED TO ME TODAY, FATHER, HELP ME DISCOVER GRATITUDE FOR ALL THE THINGS YOU'VE PROMISED.

CHOOSE GRATITUDE

Pray diligently. Stay alert,
with your eyes wide open in gratitude.
COLOSSIANS 4:2 MSG

Some people are rude and want you to be rude too. They're confused when you choose kindness—but it's God's choice, and He wants it to be yours too. When you feel like saying something you might regret, pray first, then stay alert to the consequences of being rude. Look for things to feel grateful for—you won't have to look very far.

Feelings of gratitude can be expressed simply—like thanking someone for making a delicious meal or helping you with homework and thanking God for helping you deal with hard things like feeling angry when people are rude.

Today, choose gratitude and feel thankfulness in your heart. Choose to stay alert and notice God's blessings that you usually miss. Choose to pray and let God help you do things you didn't even know were possible.

IF I EVER FEEL UNGRATEFUL, IT'S BECAUSE I HAVEN'T BEEN LOOKING FOR GOOD THINGS, GOD. HELP ME TO NOTICE ALL THE WONDERFUL THINGS YOU DO SO I CAN FEEL MORE JOY AND PEACE.

DID YOU SAY THANKS?

Praise the Lord! O give thanks to the Lord for He is good. His loving-kindness lasts forever.
PSALM 106:1 NLV

Have you ever had a great night's sleep? Did you thank God for it? When a meal was especially good, did you feel grateful to God for creating things that you can eat? Did you feel thankful the last time you took a breath or a drink of water?

To feel grateful, you'll need to pay attention to everything around you. Good things are happening; you just need to take the time to notice. Be grateful for the people who love you, the friends who stick with you, and the God who continues to walk with you. If you can walk, see, or talk, you have a reason to be grateful. If you can't—you *still* have a lot to be grateful for. Stop and think about all the things people do to help you, the love God gives you, and the things you enjoy. Then wait for gratefulness to flow from your heart.

I CAN BE GRATEFUL EVEN WHEN THINGS ARE HARD, LORD. NO MATTER WHAT I CAN'T DO, YOU CAN DO IT ALL—AND YOU LOVE ME. THANK YOU.

THANKFUL FOR EVERYTHING?

Everything God created is good, and nothing is to be rejected if it is received with thanksgiving, because it is consecrated by the word of God and prayer.

1 TIMOTHY 4:4–5 NIV

Should you feel thankful for bad days? *Yes.* How about feeling thankful for something you didn't even want? *Yes.* Thankful for hard days? *Yes.* The answer is so simple that you might have missed it when you read today's verse. *Everything* God created is good, so don't reject it. Be thankful instead.

God can use anything you face for something good. Bad doesn't have to stay bad. Sad can make room for happy. Feelings can always change, and the choice to *be* grateful can lead to *feeling* grateful. When you're grateful, you won't throw a pity party. When you have a thankful heart, you won't push people away.

Always forgive, love, and be kind. Remember that choices can change feelings. Today is always a good day for better choices that lead to better feelings.

EVEN WHEN I DON'T FEEL GRATEFUL, FATHER, HELP ME CHOOSE TO BE GRATEFUL. THANK YOU.

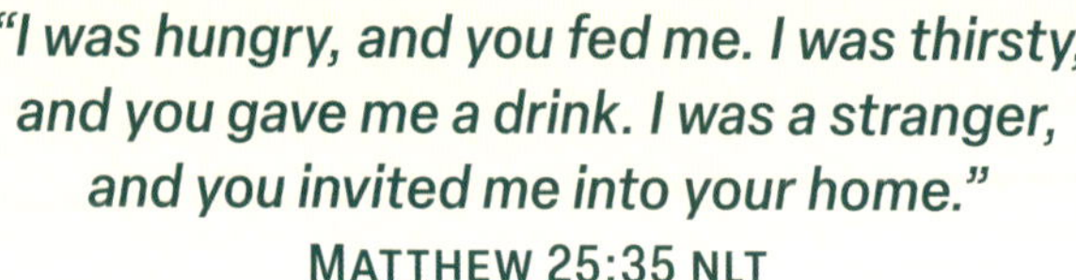

JESUS KNEW WHAT IT FELT LIKE

"I was hungry, and you fed me. I was thirsty, and you gave me a drink. I was a stranger, and you invited me into your home."

MATTHEW 25:35 NLT

Jesus described Himself as a stranger. He knew what it was like to be hungry, thirsty, and an outsider. Whatever bad feeling you've ever had, Jesus understands what it felt like.

This passage from the book of Matthew may make it seem like being a stranger is a bad thing, but truthfully, when you're a stranger, you have an opportunity to meet new people and make friends.

There was a man who did just that. He received a text message from a stranger. The message was meant for someone else. The text invited him to a holiday meal. The man replied that the text must have been a mistake. The woman who sent the text thought it was a *good* mistake. So she invited him to come to the holiday dinner with her family. He accepted the invitation and has been invited back for many years.

God doesn't want you to stay a stranger, and He wants you to help other people feel like they belong too.

JESUS CAME AS A STRANGER AND LEFT AS A FRIEND. GOD, IT'S NEVER FUN TO FEEL LIKE A STRANGER. THANKS FOR MAKING ME AN ACCEPTED PART OF YOUR FAMILY.

GOD DOESN'T WANT YOU TO STAY A STRANGER, AND HE WANTS YOU TO HELP OTHER PEOPLE FEEL LIKE THEY BELONG TOO.

A MESSAGE TO HIS FAMILY EVERYWHERE

Dear friend, you are faithful in what you are doing for the brothers and sisters, even though they are strangers to you.
3 JOHN 5 NIV

Do you know that you have something that others in countries far, far away also have? *Jesus.* These people may feel like strangers to you because you've never met them, but they're really family you just haven't met yet. Jesus made it possible for a boy like you to have family in your town, country, and world. When you help a Christian you've never met, you're sending a family member a gift.

Christians have no reason to feel like strangers when they meet other Christians. Everything they learn about God comes from the Bible—God's letter to His family *everywhere*.

When you feel like a stranger, reach out to someone who believes in Jesus. Your feelings will begin to change. Soon you'll feel like you belong.

YOU WANT THOSE WHO FOLLOW YOU TO KNOW THAT EVEN WHEN THEY FEEL LIKE A STRANGER, THEY DON'T NEED TO BE, FATHER. HELP ME MAKE FRIENDS WITH YOUR FAMILY—AFTER ALL, THEY'RE MY FAMILY TOO.

NO PEOPLE COMPARISONS

God does not see you as a Jew or as a Greek. He does not see you as a servant or as a person free to work. He does not see you as a man or as a woman. You are all one in Christ.

GALATIANS 3:28 NLV

Every person you meet is unique. Someone might have the same hair color that you have, but they might be taller—or shorter. The color of their eyes may be different from yours. The color of their skin might be a different shade. Some people use differences as excuses to avoid other people. But God said something very different. God doesn't think hair, eye, or skin color should keep people apart. God loves people no matter where they live or what they look like. There isn't a single person God loves more or less than any other. He doesn't compare people to decide who He loves most—He pays attention to the *real* you, the person you are on the inside.

THANK YOU FOR NEVER TREATING ME LIKE A STRANGER, GOD. I NEED YOUR ACCEPTANCE SO I CAN LEARN TO ACCEPT OTHERS.

YOU HAVE A FAMILY

The love of the LORD remains forever with those who fear him. His salvation extends to the children's children of those who are faithful to his covenant, of those who obey his commandments!

PSALM 103:17–18 NLT

Some people in the same family struggle to get along with each other. There can be a lot of reasons this happens, but God wants you to know that by choosing Him, you *have* a family—a *big* family! He loves His family—the ones who have chosen to be rescued and forgiven. He's kind to His family—He shows mercy and grace. He teaches His family—His words are for everyone who has accepted His gift of salvation.

When you feel like family, you understand that you're not alone. In a family, you have people who care for you and listen to you. In a family, you have people who protect you and provide for you. In a family, you always have someone who can help you learn and make better choices.

Stop questioning where you belong. When you have God, you have His family too.

THANKS FOR ALLOWING ME TO BE PART OF YOUR FAMILY, LORD. HELP ME ACCEPT OTHER FAMILY MEMBERS AND KNOW THAT I'M ALWAYS INCLUDED IN YOUR FAMILY.

PLEASE GET ALONG WITH EACH OTHER

I have a serious concern to bring up with you, my friends, using the authority of Jesus, our Master. I'll put it as urgently as I can: You must get along with each other. You must learn to be considerate of one another, cultivating a life in common.

1 CORINTHIANS 1:10 MSG

When you become part of God's family, you're asked to accept the other members of His family. It's possible that you argue with your brothers or sisters, but they're still your brothers and sisters, right? The same is true in your Christian family. God doesn't want you to fight and argue. He says, "Please get along with each other."

An adult might say the same thing to you when you fight with your brothers or sisters. God knows fighting isn't helpful. It can even stop you from learning more from Him.

Choose to get along with family—your biological family *and* God's family.

TO GET ALONG, I NEED TO LOVE YOU AND THEN LOVE OTHERS, FATHER. YOU TREAT OTHERS WITH LOVE AND KINDNESS, AND SO SHOULD I.

A FAMiLY FOR ALL

"I will be a Father to you. You will be My sons and daughters, says the All-powerful God."
2 CORINTHIANS 6:18 NLV

Some people feel sad because either they don't know their father or he's no longer living in their home. It's normal to miss someone you wish were there or to wonder about someone you've never had the chance to meet. Kids who don't have parents are sometimes called orphans. God says He loves to stay close to kids who don't have one or both parents.

When people feel lost and lonely, God says, "I will be a Father to you. You will be My sons and daughters." God will fill a hole in your heart where you need Him most. Even if you have one or both parents, God says that His gift of family is available to everyone. He wants you to know you're part of His family. How does that make you feel?

I'M GRATEFUL YOU CHOSE TO MAKE ME PART OF YOUR FAMILY, GOD. WITH YOU AS MY FATHER, I'M NEVER ALONE.

GOD'S FAMILY FEELING

"Whoever does the will of my Father in heaven is my brother and sister and mother."
MATTHEW 12:50 NIV

If you want to feel more like a member of God's family, you can do one very important thing. But before you read about that *one thing*, you need to remember what can change your feelings—the things you *choose*. So if you want to feel like part of God's family, you must *become* part of God's family. Once you accept God's gift of rescue, you should begin questioning what He wants you to do with His help.

God's family feeling starts with rescue, continues with learning, and grows with obedience. Your walk with the Lord is endlessly enriched as you stay close to His side. You can do it—because *God wants you to*. He doesn't hide what He wants you to learn. Never forget that!

I CAN SHOW OTHERS THAT I'M PART OF YOUR FAMILY, LORD. HELP ME ACCEPT YOU, LEARN FROM YOU, AND DO THE THINGS YOU ASK ME TO DO.

EMOTIONS CAN BE CONFUSING AND DIFFICULT TO HANDLE. . . ESPECIALLY WHEN YOU'RE A KID!

Whatever you're feeling, God's Word is overflowing with wisdom and advice to help you understand and manage all your moods. Anger. Sadness. Happiness. Fear. Frustration. Embarrassment. Anxiety. Confusion. Hurt. Shame. Depression. (There are so many moods!)

Big Feelings Devotions for Boys includes 200 Bible truths and prayers that will encourage and inspire you to live each day with a peaceful, contented heart.

But the fruit that comes from having the Holy Spirit in our lives is: love, joy, peace, not giving up, being kind, being good, having faith, being gentle, and being the boss over our own desires.

GALATIANS 5:22–23 NLV

Recommended for Ages 8+

Juvenile Nonfiction / Religious / Christian Devotional & Prayer

U.S. $12.99

ISBN 979-8-89151-255-9